food
between
friends

food between friends

JESSE TYLER FERGUSON
JULIE TANOUS

PHOTOGRAPHS BY EVA KOLENKO

CLARKSON POTTER/PUBLISHERS
NEW YORK

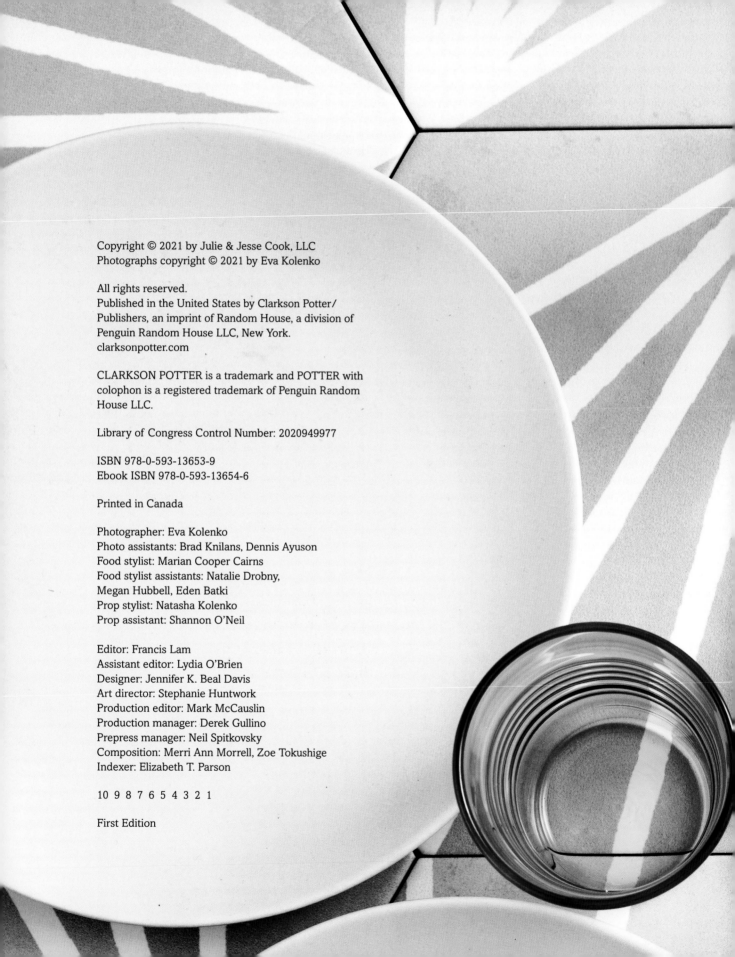

Library of Congress Control Number: 2020949977

ISBN 978-0-593-13653-9
Ebook ISBN 978-0-593-13654-6

Printed in Canada

Photographer: Eva Kolenko
Photo assistants: Brad Knilans, Dennis Ayuson
Food stylist: Marian Cooper Cairns
Food stylist assistants: Natalie Drobny,
Megan Hubbell, Eden Batki
Prop stylist: Natasha Kolenko
Prop assistant: Shannon O'Neil

Editor: Francis Lam
Assistant editor: Lydia O'Brien
Designer: Jennifer K. Beal Davis
Art director: Stephanie Huntwork
Production editor: Mark McCauslin
Production manager: Derek Gullino
Prepress manager: Neil Spitkovsky
Composition: Merri Ann Morrell, Zoe Tokushige
Indexer: Elizabeth T. Parson

10 9 8 7 6 5 4 3 2 1

First Edition

For
Josephine, Henry, and Beckett,
to whom we lovingly pass
these recipes along

contents

you guys, you have to meet my friend . . .

JESSE // I have always enjoyed creating meals for my friends and family. (Especially now that I'm a new father!) Maybe it's the need to find a creative outlet that isn't memorizing words and pretending to be other people. My favorite way to spend a free day is to crack open a few cookbooks and create a whole menu full of new recipes. I know what you're thinking and, yes, I acknowledge that my husband Justin is very lucky to be married to me. Thank you for thinking that. And you should see me in my apron embroidered with my nickname: Jesse Stewart. It was a gift from my mother-in-law, who thought I was just as good as Martha.

But let's face it, mothers-in-law are easily impressed. And the truth is, I haven't always been good at cooking. We don't need to talk about my legendary meltdown after my sixth consecutive attempt at piecrust. (You *could* earn an Oscar for re-creating it, though. Piecrust hates me! It really, really hates me!) Can we forget about the time I cooked my Thanksgiving turkey with the bag of giblets still in the bird? Or the Christmas my mother told me my homemade vanilla bean ice cream tasted like a candle?

As much as I've loved cooking, I'd always felt there was a limit to what I could do. I wanted to be one of those people who isn't intimidated about making poached eggs. I knew there must be a better way to dice an onion than the "just keep chopping it until it looks smaller" method, which I employed. And for the love of God, a piecrust really shouldn't make me cry THIS hard, should it?

It was always a dream of mine to go to culinary school, but I had this thing called a full-time job and that job was something that I not only loved but also was *actually* good at. (Good enough to receive five Emmy Award nominations. No wins, but, whatever, I'm not supposed to care about that.) I set this dream aside, a sacrifice that seemed reasonable given how truly blessed and full my life was.

Then one summer night about seven years ago I attended a friend's dinner party. Well, it wasn't just a dinner party. It had a name: "The Spring Street Social Society." As much as I wanted to support my friend, I was having a hard time getting behind this "interactive gathering" that was also short on specific details. It was being thrown at an undisclosed location; the secret address being emailed out the morning of the dinner. (Already annoying.) There was a theme. (Nope!) There was a performance. (A ukulele!) And worst of all, there was a required social-interaction element. Many things are my jam. This was not it. No, ma'am, not my jam. I settled in at the end of one of the long tables, making certain I was still within sprinting distance of the nearest exit. The Spring Street Social Society. Ay, yi, yi.

I eyed the vacant chair sitting across the table from me, praying for it to remain empty, when sure enough, right as dinner was starting, a cute girl with bangs slid into the seat. She reached a bangled hand out to me and said . . .

JULIE // "Hi, I'm Julie and I have Spring Street Social Anxiety." Those were the first words out of my mouth when I met Jesse. To my relief, he laughed. Hard!

My husband, Will, had encouraged me to attend this strange little dinner party. Our daughter Josephine was eight months old, and I was still struggling with postpartum depression and anxiety. The love I once had for cooking, eating, and meeting new people lay dormant in me, and with Will's encouragement, I was ready to shake free from it and rejoin the human race. I decided to break the ice with the redheaded human sitting across from me. Yes, I was a *Modern Family* fan and, yes, I recognized him, but in the interest of not scaring him off (he seemed just as dubious of this dinner party as I was), I played it cool. His laughter put me at ease.

We bonded over our love for food and our passion for cooking. I talked about my time at culinary school, and he asked me about my experience of being a private chef and recipe developer. We learned we both share a passion for cookbooks and we confided in each other that

we each dreamed of writing our own one day. While our fellow party guests were being forced into "conversation starter" games and singalongs, Jesse and I were plotting our first date—to cook together. Jesse had no idea what he was signing up for that night when he decided to put all his contact information in my phone.

Over the next few months we became close friends and eventually cooking partners. (We may even become lovers one day if our husbands get sick of us.) I brought my Southern roots into his kitchen with my love of sorghum syrup and passion for butter, and he brought the joys of Hatch green chiles and the art of making the perfect sopaipilla into mine. Sharing the ingredients we were raised on not only cemented our devotion to those ingredients but also cracked open a desire to learn more about their history and origins. We swapped family recipes and used them as inspiration for our own creations. I became an unpaid culinary tutor in a way, helping Jesse when he had questions about knife skills or cooking techniques. Well, I guess I was paid in amusing stories. I helped Jesse up his game in the kitchen . . .

JESSE // . . . and I taught her how to be funny on Instagram.

JULIE & JESSE // And that's basically how this book began. So, I guess the joke was on us: the Spring Street Social Society achieved just what it set out to do. Tricky bastards!

But here's the bigger thing we've discovered in our years of cooking together: anyone can learn *how* to cook, but cooking *with* someone else is a really intimate thing. It requires mutual respect, trust, and most important, chemistry. (Um, sort of like being lovers!?) It also requires a sense of humor, especially when you've reached the end of a day in the kitchen together and all you have to show for it is a wildly burnt chicken. But, hey, that's what the wine is for.

Relationships can be documented through photos and text messages, anecdotes you share, or souvenirs from travels you took together. Ours is also marked in time with this collection of recipes we have created together. They reflect not only the food we grew up eating but also the loving hands that made that food for *us*. Dishes our mothers cooked for special holidays were turned into makeover projects. (What's up with all the '80s casseroles that call for canned soup?) Restaurants we loved in our hometowns became sources of influence. Even our spouses served as inspiration: Will's Lebanese roots and Justin's fair-weather friendship with grains guided dishes we made in honor of them. (Love, honor, and fillet!) The foods our children asked for became the cornerstones

of new ideas. (Well, the food Josephine and Henry asked for, not Beckett. He is currently really into a mixture of powdered formula and water. We tried to work with those ingredients but found them pretty limiting.)

We can't wait for you to fill your kitchen with the roasting aroma of Jesse's New Mexican Red Chile Sauce (page 67) and his Hatch Green Chile Sauce (page 64). The punchy heat they bring to our Christmas Chilaquiles (page 41) is just the beginning of what their magic can do. We're excited to share a host of savory dishes that feature the golden brilliance of one of Julie's muses, sorghum syrup, such as Garlicky Sorghum Chicken Stir-Fry (page 74). We update some of our favorite childhood sweets from Biscochito

Cookie Bars (page 219) to Strawberry Semifreddo with Pretzel Crunch (page 220). You will find delicious, fresh, and boldly flavored dishes for those days you are trying to rein in the carbs (like the Citrus Baked Fish with Watercress Pesto on page 128) and *plenty* for those days when you absolutely are *not* (Fried Chicken with Crystal Hot Honey on page 47). We know you have all had the pleasure of meeting a flaky Southern-style buttermilk biscuit (and we introduce you to ours on page 198), but we are sure some of you have yet to discover the simple beauty of a New Mexican sopaipilla (see page 107). We even share a few of our favorite ways to enjoy these regional delicacies. Some people might call that micromanaging. We prefer to call it being helpful.

And, as you read and cook through this book, we hope you feel like you've made two new friends named Julie and Jesse. What better way to get to know us than through the food we love to share with each other and the stories we have built our friendship upon? Okay, no, we can't promise we will literally be your friends, but we hope the spirit of our friendship entertains and maybe even inspires you to get cooking with someone you care about.

A really great friend makes you a better person, teaching you things about yourself and expanding your imagination. A good friend cracks open your desire to learn more about yourself and the world. We can't wait to share our stories and our food with you!

some kitchen essentials

There are a few items we feel that cooks should have in their kitchens to make things easier, but we aren't going to hit you over the head with this list. (Unless it's with a **CAST-IRON PAN**—which is something you absolutely should have.) Here are what we consider essentials.

SHARP KNIVES

You think this would go without saying, but we can't tell you how many times we've cooked at a friend's house only to have to use their dull-ass knives. Nothing frustrates us more than having a ripe tomato slip out from under what is a glorified letter opener. A full knife set is great to have, but if you are going to prioritize, start with a **CHEF'S KNIFE** and a **PARING KNIFE**. (Our friend Sarah Carey also says a **SERRATED BREAD KNIFE** is essential. She works alongside Martha Stewart, so we are literally afraid to leave it off this list. And speaking of which, serrated knives are great for slicing tomatoes!) Start with these essentials and build your collection from there.

If your knives stay ready, they don't have to *get* ready! Learn how to keep those knives sharp. It's easy with a **HONING STEEL** or **ELECTRIC KNIFE SHARPENER**. And while it's not technically a knife, a pair of **KITCHEN SHEARS** is extremely helpful for cutting bones out of chicken, snipping soft herbs, or giving yourself a haircut while waiting for your oven to preheat.

MICROPLANE

Not to be confused with a tiny plane, also known as a private jet. No, a Microplane is a brand of very fine grater and a must for zesting citrus—an ingredient you will see a lot of in this book. It's also great for grating hard cheeses. (You said "hard cheeses.")

MANDOLINE

Nothing is going to slice vegetables faster and thinner than this slicer. You can buy a super-fancy one that can make several different kinds of cuts, but we prefer the simple $25 model that Benriner makes.

GARLIC PRESS

Crushing garlic with a knife is a pain in the ass. That's why some mad genius decided to invent this doodad. We use ours every day. It's worth it.

CITRUS JUICER

We like the simple "lemon yellow" and "lime green" (aren't they clever?) hand juicers that Zulay makes. Pro tip: Don't let extra citrus go bad on your counter. Juice it and freeze the juice in ice trays to use at a later date.

MORTAR AND PESTLE

We will not get off our pedestal: every kitchen needs a mortar and pestle. We also love them because they sound like a comedy duo from the 1950s. The set is perfect for grinding down whole spices or making pesto. You can use a rolling pin in a pinch, but trust us when we say the mortar and pestle is the easier option. The stone or marble kinds are the best.

THERMOMETERS

Meat thermometers are a must because "How would you like your chicken—rare or medium?" is not a question that will ever be asked. The digital kinds are so great and so easy to use. We also use a deep-fry thermometer a few times throughout this book; these thermometers (which can also double as candy thermometers) have metal clips that can be attached to the side of a pan so you don't have to stand there in agony holding it in place over hot oil or melting caramel. Ouch!

meat cook temps

- **Chicken:** The super-safe folks over at the FDA say chicken should be cooked to 165°F, but (looks over the shoulder and lowers voice) in reality 160°F or 155°F is fine as long as the chicken stays at those temperatures for a few minutes.

- **Beef:** Beef can handle a range of temperatures. Our personal preference is in the medium range, but do what is best for you. Rare: 120°F; medium-rare: 130°F; medium: 135°F; medium-well: 145°F; well-done (God help you): 155°F or until the meat looks like shoe leather. (Is it obvious that we don't like well-done beef?)

- **Pork and lamb:** Cook to at least 145°F.

OFFSET SPATULA

Think of this as a large, gentle butter knife. It's not only the best tool for frosting cakes but is also perfect for gently coaxing muffins out of their tins or gently flipping smaller pieces of food.

COOLING RACKS

Wire cooling racks are slightly elevated and vital for keeping baked goods off the counter to allow air to circulate under them. Otherwise, the bottom of that yellow cake will be ruined.

DRY AND LIQUID MEASURING CUPS

Apologies if we're preaching to the choir, but we can't tell you how many times we've witnessed people (who will remain nameless) measuring dry ingredients (like flour and sugar) in a liquid measuring cup and vice versa. In *theory*, they measure the same amounts, but dry cups are meant to be filled to the top and leveled off; good luck doing that with water and not spilling it. And liquid cups should have spouts for pouring and lines to measure by sight.

If we can add one more thought here: think of measuring spoons and cups as training wheels. They are great tools for controlling the seasoning when you are learning how to cook. Our recipes have been well tested, but everyone's palate is different. Learn what a tablespoon of spice looks like in the palm of your hand, and challenge yourself to cook without methodically measuring everything. Your taste buds will tell you if you need more spice or acidity or salt. If you love garlic and a recipe calls for only a touch, feel free to add more! If you hate cilantro, leave it out! The world will not stop spinning, we promise.

But, for baking, disregard everything we just said. Measurements are key in baking, and recipes don't offer much wiggle room. Think of baking as chemistry class. It's important to be precise.

mise en place

One of the best tools for being successful in the kitchen doesn't cost you anything but a little time. It is just the extra effort it takes to properly set up your workspace. Now, because the French like to make everything sound fancy, they have given this activity a name: *mise en place*. It means "everything in its place," but for us it translates to "getting your shit together." You know how, when you watch a cooking show, Martha or Rachael or Snoop Dogg always has all the ingredients premeasured, chopped, and in little bowls? That is mise en place. (Yes, they have production assistants who do it for them, but you can do it, too.)

Take the time before you start to read through the entire recipe, assemble your tools, and get your ingredients prepped and ready. This can sometimes take even longer than the active cook time, but it's *so* worth it! Preparing your space and your ingredients without the stress of a ticking clock or the threat of something burning in a pan is not only going to make your time in the kitchen more enjoyable, but it will also make it more efficient. You won't accidentally swap baking powder for baking soda because you are working too fast. You will avoid countless mistakes this way, and it is the surest means for achieving success in the kitchen. (The next best way would be to just let Martha or Rachael or Snoop Dogg do the work while you sit back and relax.)

OPTIONAL (BUT VERY NICE)

Okay, these next few items are a little more expensive than mise en place (which is basically free). If you don't want to get them for yourself, don't worry. You can still use this book, and we still respect you and see a future in this relationship. You can also consider requesting these for your next birthday, holiday, or push present.*

STAND MIXER

Yes, it is possible to bake without a stand mixer (a hand mixer is a great tool that we also use a lot), but KitchenAid stand mixers certainly make our lives ealus they're attractive enough to live on your counter and serve as a constant reminder that it's never a bad time to whip up a batch of cookies. (Or at least make you feel like the type of person who would spontaneously whip up a batch of cookies.)

DUTCH OVEN

Here's another item that's pretty enough to display. These heavy-bottomed pots are life-changers (we acknowledge how dramatic we sound right now), and we use ours every day. The enameled cast-iron pots can be transferred from stovetop to oven and are big enough to handle everything from roasts to soups. There are a lot of good ones on the market, but our favorites are made by Le Creuset, Staub, and Great Jones. Pick your favorite color and leave it on the stovetop so it's always ready to roll!

*Jesse here. Julie just told me what a "push present" is. I had no idea. It's a gift a partner gives to a woman before giving birth. I have so many questions, but the one I really want an answer to is: What if it's a Caesarean birth? Also, I don't know if a blender, even if it is a Vitamix, is the proper gift in exchange for bringing a human into the world.

A GOOD BLENDER

When we were kids, a blender was used for one thing: milkshakes. Now we use them for soups, pestos, dressings, marinades, quick sauces, and yes, margaritas. If you can swing it, get a high-speed Vitamix, but any model with speed settings works.

FOOD PROCESSOR

These just make food prep so much easier. Also, we can't make piecrust anymore without one. I mean we can, but we really, really, really don't want to. At least Jesse doesn't.

ONE LAST THING . . . SALT

We need to discuss salt. There isn't a single recipe in this cookbook that calls for iodized salt. Also referred to as table salt, iodized salt is no doubt the kind that many of our parents used when we were growing up, but the thing is: it isn't the best to cook with. It isn't terribly delicious (iodized = iodine flavor), and it doesn't have the same nice texture as kosher salt.

Our favorite kosher salt is made by Diamond Crystal, and it is the one we used to develop and test these recipes. The other leading brand for kosher salt (do we sound like a diaper commercial?) is Morton. Here is the crazy thing about these two brands of kosher salt: Diamond Crystal and Morton are nearly 40 percent off from each other in terms of saltiness. Just know that Morton kosher salt is the saltier of the two. (We know—who thought salt would end up being the ingredient that was so complicated?)

If you're using salt only to taste, then it doesn't really matter which kosher salt you use. But in our recipes, when we call for a measured amount of salt, that means we used that much Diamond Crystal salt in testing the recipe. If you're using Morton, reduce that specified amount of salt by one-third or one-half, or else your food may come out too salty.

Here's a funny side story: A few years ago, Diamond Crystal discontinued one of its package sizes of kosher salt. The news went viral online and like most things on the internet, when people got hold of it, they completely twisted the story and launched a rumor that the company was discontinuing its kosher salt entirely. Our editor, Francis "Believes Everything He Reads on the Internet" Lam told Chrissy "Loves Her Diamond Crystal" Teigen (whose cookbooks he also edits) that she had better stock up before the salt was gone forever. We caught wind of it when Chrissy took to Twitter to share the news with her 30 million followers. It was like an insane game of telephone. Needless to say, it was all a giant misunderstanding and Diamond Crystal is still readily available, even though Chrissy and Francis bought substantial amounts in a panic.

brunch: not just a sunday thing

Can we please start a petition to make brunch the new "most important meal of the day"? We all love that special Sunday meal, so why not extend it to the other six days of the week? These recipes are going to take a little more effort than scrambled eggs, but we assume you are up for the challenge because you bought this book. From a potluck gathering to a decadent midweek treat, these delectable dishes will have your friends and family saying, "Thanks a brunch!"

green shakshuka

blue cornmeal pancakes

I wish I could say that I always knew about blue corn, as it's indigenous to the Southwest and was an option in virtually every New Mexican restaurant in Albuquerque, but here's the truth: Disney's *Pocahontas* first exposed me to it. I had never "heard the wolf cry to the blue corn moon," but my interest was piqued! Blue corn? What, where, when, why, *and* how? I learned that blue corn can be traced back to the Pueblo Native American Indian tribes in New Mexico, and with its slightly sweet flavor and dusty blue hue it is one of the region's most beautiful and cherished ingredients. The next time I noticed it on a menu, I went for it. It felt fancy *and* it was referenced in an Oscar-winning song. There is a whole scientific explanation as to why blue corn is blue, but I seem to have used up all my space talking about my love for *Pocahontas*. Just know that these crunchy pancakes are a tribute to that unique taste from my childhood—and to Judy Kuhn*. ~Jesse

1½ cups **blue cornmeal**
¼ cup **all-purpose flour**
1 tablespoon **sugar**
1½ teaspoons **baking powder**
½ teaspoon **baking soda**
¼ teaspoon **kosher salt**
2 large **eggs**, lightly beaten

1½ cups **buttermilk**
¼ cup **canola or grapeseed oil**
Nonstick cooking spray
Blueberry Butter (page 264)
Maple syrup

1. In a large bowl, whisk together the cornmeal, flour, sugar, baking powder, baking soda, and salt.

2. In a medium bowl or large liquid measuring cup, whisk together the eggs, buttermilk, and oil until smooth.

3. Make a well in the center of the dry ingredients and pour in the buttermilk mixture. Use a rubber spatula or wooden spoon to fold together until just combined. Do not overmix. Allow the batter to rest for about 5 minutes.

4. Heat a griddle or large nonstick skillet over medium-high heat and grease lightly with nonstick cooking spray. Pour or scoop the batter onto the griddle, using 2 heaping tablespoons of batter for each pancake. With the back of the spoon, gently spread the batter into a 3- to 4-inch circle. Cook until golden brown, about 3 minutes. Flip and cook on the other side until golden brown and the center of the pancake feels slightly firm to the touch, another 3 minutes. Remove from the pan and repeat with the remaining batter.

5. Serve the pancakes hot with the blueberry butter and maple syrup.

*Judy Kuhn is a brilliant Broadway actor who also just happens to be the singing voice of Pocahontas. It should also be noted that Vanessa Williams did a great job with the pop version of the song, which played over the closing credits.

little grits soufflés

MAKES 12 LITTLE SOUFFLÉS

Chef Frank Stitt is a legend in Alabama, and his signature appetizer of individual ramekin-baked grits are out of this world. When I think about grits, I think about Frank. Even though my hometown of Cullman, Alabama, was a mere forty miles from his Birmingham restaurant, Highlands Bar and Grill, in my eyes it might as well have been as far away as Paris. I adored how he celebrated the food I grew up eating while lovingly lifting it up.

In this recipe, I literally (and lovingly) lift grits up by making a bowl of cheese grits puff up in the oven with the help of some whipped eggs. Living outside of the South makes it a little harder to find real stone-ground grits, so I love that these little soufflés work best with the quick-cooking variety, which can be found almost anywhere. I've even seen them at larger drugstores that sell pantry items (like premixed margaritas). I know, I know—any self-respecting Southerner should stay away from quick-cooking grits, but sometimes that's all you can find. Please forgive me, Frank Stitt!

Like many delightful things—party balloons, air mattresses, and good moods—these soufflés will eventually deflate, so enjoy them while they are fluffy and fun. ~ Julie

Nonstick cooking spray
2 cups **whole milk**
½ cup **quick-cooking white grits**
1 teaspoon **kosher salt**
Freshly ground black pepper
1 cup finely grated **sharp cheddar cheese** (3½ ounces)
1 tablespoon **unsalted butter**
4 large **eggs**

EQUIPMENT
12-cup muffin tin or 12 small ramekins

1. Preheat the oven to 375°F. Coat a 12-cup muffin tin or 12 small ramekins with nonstick cooking spray.

2. Bring the milk to a simmer in a medium saucepan over medium heat. Reduce the heat to medium low and whisk in the grits, a little at a time, until incorporated. Bring to a simmer, cover, and cook, stirring occasionally, until thick and creamy, about 10 minutes. Remove the pot from the heat and stir in the salt, pepper, cheese, and butter until smooth. Transfer to a large bowl and allow to cool for about 5 minutes.

3. Meanwhile, separate the egg yolks and whites. Add the egg yolks to a small bowl and lightly beat with a fork. Place the egg whites in the bowl of a stand mixer fitted with the whisk attachment. Beat the egg whites on medium-high speed until they hold firm, stiff peaks, 2 to 3 minutes.

4. Gradually add the beaten yolks to the grits, mixing well between each addition.

5. Gently fold one-third of the egg whites into the grits mixture, rotating the bowl, until incorporated. Repeat with another third of the egg whites, and then the last third. Use an ice cream scoop to fill the muffin cups or ramekins almost to the top with the batter. Bake until the soufflés rise and are golden brown on top, about 25 minutes. Serve immediately.

deep-dish chorizo quiche

When I was growing up, gay characters on TV (of which there weren't many) would always be making quiche, for some reason. I don't know if Mitch and Cam actually ever *made* one of these custardy, savory treats, but I am 100 percent sure we referenced it at some point. So, as part of the graduating class of Gay Television Characters, I feel it is my duty to share my favorite quiche recipe with you.

It's also worth noting that my friend Danielle thought *quiche* was pronounced quick-ee. I learned this when I was having brunch with her and she told our (very handsome) waiter, "I think I'll be fine with just the quickie today." ~ **Jesse**

CRUST

1½ cups **all-purpose flour**

½ teaspoon **kosher salt**

½ cup (1 stick) **unsalted butter**, cut into dice and chilled in freezer for at least 20 minutes

4 to 5 tablespoons **ice water**

FILLING

1 tablespoon **olive oil**

1 **garlic clove**, minced

1 medium **shallot**, finely chopped

8 ounces **raw chorizo sausage** (3 links), casings removed

6 jarred mild **Peppadew peppers**, drained and chopped (about ¾ cup)

1 cup chopped **fresh parsley**

7 large **eggs**

1 cup **whole milk**

½ cup **heavy cream**

½ teaspoon **celery salt**

¼ teaspoon **celery seeds**

⅛ teaspoon **ground white pepper**

Pinch of **ground nutmeg**

½ teaspoon **kosher salt**

½ to ¾ cup grated 3-month-aged **Manchego cheese**, or **Monterey jack, cheddar,** or **mozzarella**

EQUIPMENT

9-inch deep-dish pie pan (see Note, page 26)

1. Make the crust: Add the flour and salt to the bowl of a food processor and pulse to combine. Add the cold butter and pulse until incorporated and the flour looks like coarse meal, about 15 pulses. Drizzle in 4 tablespoons of the ice water and pulse until the dough just comes together, adding more water, 1 teaspoon at a time, as needed. Turn the dough out onto a clean surface and shape into a disc. Wrap in plastic wrap and refrigerate until ready to use, at least 1 hour.

2. Preheat the oven to 400°F.

3. Roll the dough out to a 13-inch round. Using the rolling pin, carefully transfer the dough to a 9-inch deep-dish pie pan, gently lowering the edges of the dough so it falls flush against the bottom and sides of the pan. Crimp the edges as desired. Line the dough with a sheet of foil or parchment paper. Fill with pie weights or dried beans and bake until the edges feel firm and are just turning golden, 20 to 25 minutes. Remove from the oven, carefully remove the pie weights and foil, and let the crust cool while you make the filling. Reduce the oven temperature to 350°F.

recipe continues . . .

1. In a large skillet, heat the oil over medium heat until hot and shimmering. Add the garlic and shallot and sauté until soft, about 1 minute. Add the chorizo and cook, breaking up with a wooden spoon, until cooked through, about 3 minutes. Add the Peppadews and cook for another minute, until warmed through. Remove the pan from the heat and stir in the parsley.

5. In a medium bowl, whisk together the eggs, milk, cream, celery salt, celery seed, white pepper, nutmeg, and salt. Stir in the cheese.

6. Place the pie pan on a baking sheet. Scrape the chorizo mixture into the crust, then pour the custard over the top. It should come to just below the crimping.

7. Bake, rotating the pan halfway through, until the quiche is just set and no longer jiggly in the center, 50 to 60 minutes. Remove from the oven and let cool for about 5 minutes. Slice and serve, or keep covered in the refrigerator for 3 to 4 days. (To reheat, bring the quiche out of the refrigerator and let come to room temperature. Place on a baking sheet, cover with foil, and heat in a 350°F oven for about 15 minutes, until warmed through.)

---

note

If you don't have a deep-dish pie pan, stop panicking and get ready for some good news. You, lucky devil, will have some filling left over. Store it in the fridge and scramble it in a skillet the next morning!

sweet & sticky orange cardamom rolls

The All Steak Restaurant—which first opened its doors in 1938—is famous in Cullman, Alabama, but not necessarily for their steaks. With a cigarette vending machine that was always well stocked and located conveniently by the entrance, the All Steak was where people congregated at 7:00 a.m. to smoke cigarettes and discuss politics, and it was where friends and couples met at 6:00 p.m. to smoke more cigarettes and forget the day's troubles—and to eat orange rolls, which were on the house! I guess the cigarette vending machine at the entrance made them enough money that they didn't need to charge people for their orange rolls. Eighty-two years later, the orange rolls still taste just as delicious today. I love them so much that I cold-called the restaurant and spoke to Dyron, the current owner, about the original recipe. I created this recipe to carry the spirit of the rolls I grew up eating. Plus, it's cheaper than buying a round-trip ticket to Alabama. Few things in life are free, but the orange rolls still are, thanks to Dyron! ~ Julie

DOUGH

1½ cups plus 1 tablespoon **all-purpose flour**

2 tablespoons **granulated sugar**

1 teaspoon (½ packet) **instant yeast**

½ teaspoon **kosher salt**

¼ teaspoon **ground cardamom**

¼ cup **whole milk**

2 tablespoons **fresh orange juice**, strained to remove pulp

3 tablespoons **unsalted butter**, melted, plus some more for greasing

1 **egg**, beaten, room temperature

FILLING

5 tablespoons **unsalted butter**, room temperature

¼ cup **granulated sugar**

½ tablespoon finely grated **orange zest** (from ½ large orange)

⅛ teaspoon (2 pinches) **ground cardamom**

GLAZE

1 cup **confectioners' sugar**

1 tablespoon **unsalted butter**, melted

¾ teaspoon finely grated **orange zest**

1½ to 2 tablespoons **fresh orange juice**

EQUIPMENT

12-cup muffin tin

Paper liners

Nonstick cooking spray

1. Make the dough: In the bowl of a stand mixer, whisk together the flour, sugar, yeast, salt, and cardamom. In a medium bowl or large liquid measuring cup, whisk together the milk and orange juice. Microwave until heated to 100° to 115°F, about 20 seconds.

Add the 3 tablespoons melted butter and the egg to the wet ingredients and whisk to combine. Pour the wet ingredients into the dry ingredients.

2. Fit the hook attachment onto the stand mixer and knead the dough on medium-low speed until it just comes together, 1 minute. Increase the speed to medium and knead until the dough is smooth and pulls away from the bottom of the bowl, another 4 to 5 minutes. Remove the dough from the bowl and gently shape into a ball. Lightly grease the

recipe continues . . .

bottom of the stand mixer bowl with some melted butter and place the dough back in the bowl, flipping the ball of dough to coat it on all sides with the butter. Cover with plastic wrap and let rise in a warm, draft-free place until almost doubled in size, 60 to 75 minutes.

3. **Make the filling:** In a medium bowl, mash together the butter, sugar, orange zest, and cardamom until well combined.

4. Line a 12-cup muffin tin with paper liners and lightly spray the liners with nonstick cooking spray.

5. On a floured surface, roll out the dough to ⅛ inch thick, about 12 x 12 inches. Spread the filling evenly over the dough. Roll the dough up as tightly as you can into a 12-inch log. Using a sharp, serrated knife and a light touch, trim about ½ inch off of either end and discard. Then slice the dough into 12 pieces, each just shy of an inch thick.

6. Place the rolls in the muffin cups, cover with plastic wrap, and let rise until puffed, 30 minutes.

7. Preheat the oven to 375°F. Arrange a rack in the center of the oven.

8. Bake the rolls until light golden brown and the dough is cooked through, 12 to 15 minutes.

9. **Make the glaze:** In a medium bowl, whisk together the confectioners' sugar, melted butter, orange zest, and 1½ tablespoons of the orange juice until smooth and pourable, adding more juice as needed, 1 teaspoon at a time, to reach your desired consistency.

10. Remove the rolls from the oven and spoon 1 tablespoon of glaze over each roll while still warm. Let cool for a couple of minutes before serving.

flossin'

When slicing delicate doughs that you don't want to squish down too much, even better than a serrated knife is to use dental floss! You can loop it around the dough and give it a firm pull, and it slices cleanly. Just make sure you're using unwaxed and unflavored floss, though!

green shakshuka

In the past, when I've hosted brunch, I tried to make everyone omelets, which for me can be a time-consuming disaster. That's when I tried my first shakshuka . . . and, honey, you'll always remember your first shakshuka. Popular in Arab, North African, and Mediterranean cuisines, shakshuka is a rich, savory breakfast dish of tomatoey stewed vegetables, often made in a skillet with eggs on top. All you have to do is scoop out the servings, pour yourself a mimosa, and enjoy your guests. (Assuming you like them.) For our version, we brought in some Alabama and New Mexico, with collard greens and green chiles. (And this has nothing to do with the recipe, but as I was writing this, my computer autocorrected "shakshuka" to "Shakira" every single time.) ~ **Jesse**

6 tablespoons **heavy cream**

¼ cup **buttermilk**

¼ cup **olive oil**

1 medium **white onion**, diced

2 **celery stalks**, diced

2 **garlic cloves**, minced

½ teaspoon **celery seeds**

2 medium **tomatillos** or **fresh green tomatoes**, chopped

1 pound **fresh collard greens, mustard greens,** or **kale** (about 1 large bunch), stemmed and roughly chopped

½ cup **chicken broth, vegetable broth,** or **potlikker** (see page 179)

2 tablespoons canned diced **Hatch green chiles**

1 cup chopped **fresh soft herbs**, such as parsley, dill, chives, and/or **scallions**, plus more scallions for garnish

4 sprigs of **fresh thyme**, leaves stripped off

Kosher salt and **freshly ground black pepper**

6 large **eggs**

Toast or **Buttermilk Biscuits** (page 198)

1. Preheat the broiler. Pull out the cream and buttermilk from the refrigerator so they can come to room temperature; this will prevent them from curdling when added to the hot pan.

2. Heat the oil in a large, heavy-bottomed skillet with high sides over medium heat until hot and shimmering. Add the onion and celery and cook until softened and just turning golden, 8 minutes. Add the garlic and celery seeds and cook until fragrant, 1 minute. Increase the heat to medium high and add the tomatillos and the greens and cook until just wilted, about 5 minutes. Pour in the broth and cook until the liquid is mostly evaporated, about 4 minutes, then stir in the chiles, herbs, and thyme leaves. Season to taste with salt and pepper. Reduce the heat to medium low and stir in the cream. Cook until the liquid thickens, 2 to 3 minutes, then stir in the buttermilk. Season to taste with more salt and pepper.

3. Use the back of a ladle or spoon to make 6 wells in the greens mixture. Crack the eggs, one at a time, into a small ramekin, then gently transfer to a well, taking care not to break the yolks. Cook on the stovetop for 2 to 3 minutes, then transfer the skillet to the oven and broil until the egg whites are just opaque and the yolks are still runny, about 3 minutes.

4. Garnish the shakshuka with more scallions and serve hot with toast or biscuits alongside.

baklava french toast

When Jesse and I go out for breakfast, French toast is consistently the dish that mocks us from a neighboring table while we sit miserable with our scrambled eggs and avocado. (It's *always* Jesse's idea to go for the healthy option, and I *always* foolishly follow his lead.)

It is hard to improve upon a nearly perfect thing, but this nut-and-honey version (inspired by my husband Will's Lebanese roots and his love of baklava) has us doing poor-form cartwheels! This orange-honey syrup would make a bee weak in the knees, while the panko bread crumbs and chopped nuts give that bread a perfect texture and crunch. Three cheers for baklava! Hip, Hip, Lava! ~Julie

Orange-Honey Syrup
(recipe follows)

½ cup **whole milk**

6 large **eggs**

2 pinches of **ground cloves**

1 teaspoon **kosher salt**

4 teaspoons **vanilla extract**

1 cup finely chopped **pistachios** and **walnuts**

1 cup **plain panko bread crumbs**

8 (1-inch-thick) slices of **challah, brioche bread,** or **pullman bread**

4 to 6 tablespoons **unsalted butter**

1. In a shallow bowl or baking dish, whisk together ½ cup of the orange-honey syrup, the milk, eggs, a pinch of cloves, the salt, and vanilla.

2. In another shallow dish, toss together the chopped nuts, panko, and remaining pinch of cloves.

3. Place 2 or 3 bread slices in the milk mixture, turning to coat well. Let the bread soak for 1 to 2 minutes, depending on the type of bread you're using (sliced brioche won't be able to handle a long soak). Remove the bread from the milk soak, one slice at a time, and transfer to the dish with the nut mixture. Press gently to adhere the dry mixture to both sides of the bread.

4. In a large pan, melt 2 to 3 tablespoons of the butter over medium heat. When the butter is hot and starting to bubble, add the bread to the pan, 2 or 3 slices at a time, or as many will fit without overcrowding. Cook the bread until golden and toasty on one side, 4 to 5 minutes. Flip and cook on the other side until golden brown and toasty, another 4 to 5 minutes. Transfer to a platter while you repeat steps 3 and 4 with the remaining bread slices, using the remaining 2 to 3 tablespoons butter.

5. Serve the French toast warm with the syrup.

orange–honey syrup

MAKES 1¼ CUPS

¼ cup **honey**

¾ cup **light brown sugar**

¾ cup **water**

1 tablespoon finely
grated **orange zest**
(from 1 large orange)

3 tablespoons **fresh
orange juice**, strained
to remove pulp

2 teaspoons **ground
cinnamon**

1½ tablespoons **vanilla
extract**

6 tablespoons (¾ stick)
unsalted butter, cut
into dice

In a small saucepan, whisk together the honey,
brown sugar, water, orange zest, orange
juice, and cinnamon. Bring to a simmer
over medium-high heat, about 2 minutes.
Reduce the heat to medium and cook at a
gentle simmer, whisking occasionally, until
thickened slightly and reduced to ¾ cup, 15 to
17 minutes. Whisk in the vanilla and butter
until the butter is melted and the syrup is
glossy. Remove the pan from the heat and
cover to keep warm until ready to use.

apple–cheddar drop biscuits

MAKES
15 TO 18
BISCUITS

A wise person once said, "An apple pie without cheese is like a kiss without the squeeze." Yes, we know this isn't a pie recipe, but we think that rule still applies.

It's totally understandable why people put slices of cheese on their apple pie: sweet, savory, salty, tart, buttery. This biscuit hits all the same spots, and it's the perfect "starter biscuit" for baking beginners, like Jesse was. No kneading! No rolling! Just spooning and dropping! They are almost impossible to mess up. We say "almost" because we don't want a lawsuit if you do actually mess them up. ~ Julie

2¼ cups **all-purpose flour**, plus more for dusting

2½ teaspoons **baking powder**

1 tablespoon **sugar**

1 teaspoon **kosher salt**

10 tablespoons (1¼ sticks) **unsalted butter**, cut into ¼-inch dice and chilled in the freezer for at least 20 minutes

6 ounces **sharp cheddar cheese**, grated on the large holes of a box grater (about 1½ cups), chilled

1 **Granny Smith** or **Honeycrisp apple**, peeled, cored, and cut into ¼-inch dice

1 cup cold **buttermilk**

1. Preheat the oven to 400°F. Line 2 baking sheets with parchment paper.

2. In a large bowl, whisk together the flour, baking powder, sugar, and salt. Add the butter and use your fingers or a pastry cutter to pinch and incorporate the butter into the dry ingredients until the mixture resembles coarse crumbs, working quickly so the butter remains cold. Fold in the grated cheese and diced apple. Drizzle in the buttermilk and fold with a rubber spatula until just combined and most of the dry, floury bits are incorporated, but do not overmix. The dough will be shaggy and sort of sticky.

3. Scoop out ¼ cup of the biscuit dough and gently shape it into a loose mound. If the dough feels too sticky, lightly dust your hands with flour.

Place it on the prepared baking sheet, then shape and place the remaining dough mounds on the sheets, spacing about 1 inch apart. Bake the biscuits, rotating the sheets halfway through, until the tops are golden brown in spots and the biscuits feel somewhat firm to the touch, 15 to 18 minutes. Transfer to a wire rack and allow the biscuits to cool for about 5 minutes before serving.

buckwheat waffles

For some reason, Justin loves breakfast in bed. I know, weird. Who wants to lie in bed on a Sunday morning with the dogs while someone else makes you waffles and a mimosa with fresh-squeezed orange juice and then brings it up to you on a tray with a flower? Just Justin—and I assume the Queen of England. Waffles to me are always a Sunday-morning luxury. I can't remember ever making waffles on a weekday, although I can't remember a weekday in which I didn't crave them. These waffles carry a secret super power: cottage cheese. It's mild in flavor so it's almost undetectable, but the curds still are able to work their magic, creating tiny pockets of creaminess.

To me, waffles have always been about what you put on top of them, and as much as I adore this buckwheat version, I didn't want it to miss out on the topping party. Sweet and tart lemon curd dotted with poppy seeds works beautifully with our slightly chunky walnut butter. If you are feeling slightly chunky yourself after indulging in these waffles, remind yourself that buckwheat is a protein-packed nutritious grain that promotes good health! You can also tell yourself that waffles are just pancakes with abs. Don't have a waffle maker? No worries, you can cook this batter on a griddle to make pancakes as well! ~ **Jesse**

2 large **eggs**, whites and yolks separated

1½ cups **buckwheat flour**; or ½ cup **whole wheat flour** and 1 cup **all-purpose flour**

2 teaspoons **baking powder**

½ teaspoon **baking soda**

½ teaspoon **kosher salt**

1 tablespoon **poppy seeds**

6 tablespoons (¾ stick) **unsalted butter**, melted

¼ cup **light brown sugar**

1 teaspoon **vanilla extract**

Finely grated **zest and juice of 1 lemon**

½ cup **full-fat cottage cheese**

¾ cup **whole milk**

Walnut-Honey Butter (page 264)

Poppy Seed Lemon Curd (recipe follows)

1. Preheat a waffle iron to medium-high heat.

2. Place the egg whites in a medium bowl or in the bowl of a stand mixer. Using an electric hand mixer or the stand mixer with the whisk attachment, whip the egg whites on medium speed until they hold stiff peaks, about 5 minutes.

3. In a large bowl, whisk together the flour, baking powder, baking soda, salt, and poppy seeds. In a medium bowl, whisk together the egg yolks, melted butter, brown sugar, vanilla, lemon zest and juice, cottage cheese, and milk until well combined. Add the wet ingredients to the dry ingredients and gently stir until just incorporated. Gently fold the whipped egg whites into the batter until just incorporated. Do not overmix!

4. Every waffle maker is different so, following the manufacturer's instructions, pour the designated amount of batter into the waffle maker and cook until golden brown. Repeat with the remaining batter.

5. Serve the waffles warm, topped with a dollop of walnut butter and lemon curd. (Leftover waffles will keep in the refrigerator for up to 1 week or in the freezer for up to 3 months. Reheat in a toaster, "Leggo my Eggo"–style!)

poppy seed lemon curd

MAKES ABOUT 2 CUPS

Finely grated **zest of 1 lemon**
¾ cup **fresh lemon juice**
¾ cup **sugar**
3 large **eggs**

½ cup (1 stick) **unsalted butter**, cut into chunks
2 teaspoons **poppy seeds**

In a small saucepan, whisk together the lemon zest and juice, sugar, and eggs until the sugar dissolves. Turn the heat to medium low and cook, whisking constantly so the eggs don't scramble, until thickened, 10 to 15 minutes. Add the butter and whisk until melted and smooth, about 3 minutes more. Pour the curd into a glass jar or heatproof bowl, straining through a fine-mesh sieve if lumps have formed. Stir in the poppy seeds. Let cool to room temperature; the curd will continue to thicken. (The lemon curd will keep in an airtight container in the refrigerator for up to 1 week.)

oatmeal cream pie muffins

No brunch buffet is complete without muffins, or as my kids like to call them, breakfast cupcakes. I couldn't help myself here and I made a lightly sweetened cream cheese frosting to spread on top. If I am making these for a Sunday brunch I always frost them. They are a delicious and decadent weekend treat reminiscent of an oatmeal cream pie. If I am making them for a weekday grab-and-go breakfast, I leave the icing off. Okay, I'm lying. I make the frosting and keep it in a container in the fridge—sometimes it's gone before the unfrosted muffins are. ~ Julie

¾ cup **old-fashioned rolled oats**

⅔ cup **oat milk, whole milk**, or **buttermilk**

1 cup **all-purpose flour**

1½ tablespoons **cocoa powder**

2 teaspoons **baking powder**

½ teaspoon **kosher salt**

¼ teaspoon **baking soda**

1 tablespoon **ground cinnamon**

2¼ teaspoons **ground ginger**

⅛ teaspoon **ground nutmeg**

⅔ cup **canola oil**

½ cup **light brown sugar**

3 tablespoons **unsulfured molasses, sorghum syrup**, or **golden syrup**

1 tablespoon **vanilla extract**

2 large **eggs**, room temperature

½ cup chopped **walnuts** or **pecans** (optional)

Cream Cheese Frosting (recipe follows)

EQUIPMENT

12-cup muffin tin

Paper liners or nonstick cooking spray

1. Place a rack in the center of the oven. Preheat the oven to 350°F. Line the muffin cups with paper liners or coat with nonstick cooking spray.

2. Add ½ cup of the oats to the milk, stir to combine, and let the oats soak for 10 minutes.

3. In the bowl of a food processor, pulse the remaining ¼ cup oats until finely ground. Add the flour, cocoa powder, baking powder, salt, baking soda, cinnamon, ginger, and nutmeg. Pulse a few times until thoroughly combined.

4. In a large bowl, whisk together the oil, brown sugar, molasses, and vanilla until well combined and emulsified. Add the eggs, one at a time, whisking between each addition. Using a rubber spatula, stir in half the dry ingredients, then the milk-soaked oats, then the remaining dry ingredients. Stir until just combined; do not overmix. Fold in the nuts, if using.

5. Use a spring-loaded ice cream scoop or spoon to divide the batter among the muffin

cups, filling them almost to the top. Bake for about 20 minutes, or until a toothpick inserted in the center of a muffin comes out mostly clean, with some moist crumbs still stuck to the toothpick. Transfer the muffin tin to a wire rack and allow to cool for 2 minutes. Carefully tilt the tin to pop out the muffins and allow them to cool for 5 to 10 more minutes on the rack.

6. Spread the cream cheese frosting on top of the muffins and serve.

cream cheese frosting

MAKES ABOUT 1 CUP

½ cup (1 stick) **unsalted butter**, room temperature

4 ounces (½ cup) **cream cheese**, room temperature

2 teaspoons **vanilla extract**

½ cup **confectioners' sugar**, sifted

1. In a medium bowl, beat together the butter, cream cheese, and vanilla with an electric hand mixer until smooth. Gradually add the confectioners' sugar and beat until smooth.

2. Use the frosting immediately or store in the refrigerator in an airtight container for up to 1 week. Bring it to room temperature before spreading on the muffins.

christmas chilaquiles

SERVES
4 TO 6

"Red, green, or Christmas?" is a common question when ordering New Mexican food in Albuquerque. Class, what do you think "Christmas" means? Bueller? Bueller? Bueller? That's right! It means both red and green chiles, and they turn your plate into a beautiful, saucy, holiday-colored explosion of flavor. Chiles are the umami of the Southwest.

New Mexican cuisine is a perfect fusion of Pueblo Native American and traditional Mexican fare. Its emphasis on local spices, herbs, and chiles (both red and green) sets its flavors apart. Chilaquiles, a crunchy and soft tortilla-chip stew, is an ancient Mexican dish—the name comes from the Nahuatl language that predates Spanish in Mexico! We give this traditional dish a "New Mexcellent" spin with both red and green chile sauce.

P.S.: Yes, it's *chile* with an *e* at the end, not an *i*, when speaking of the pepper. Don't @ us.

P.P.S. If you were being super authentic, you would fry tortillas first, but for simplicity's sake, we use store-bought tortilla chips. ~ Jesse

2 tablespoons **olive oil**
1 medium **onion**, diced
1 medium **jalapeño**, seeded and diced
2 **garlic cloves**, minced
2 cups **New Mexican Red Chile Sauce** (page 67)
2 cups **chicken** or **vegetable broth**
Kosher salt and freshly **ground black pepper**
6 large **eggs**

2 tablespoons finely chopped **fresh cilantro**, plus more for garnish
1 (9-ounce) bag **tortilla chips**
1 cup **Hatch Green Chile Sauce** (page 64)
1 **avocado**, sliced or diced
Mexican crema or **sour cream**

1. In a large, heavy-bottomed pot or Dutch oven, heat 1 tablespoon of the olive oil over medium heat until shimmering. Add the onion and jalapeño and sauté until soft, 4 to 5 minutes. Add the garlic and cook until fragrant, about 2 minutes. Add the red chile sauce. Bring to a simmer and cook for 3 to 4 minutes, until slightly thickened. Add the broth, let it return to a simmer, then reduce the heat to medium low and continue to simmer for 10 minutes, until reduced slightly to the consistency of a thin sauce. Remove the pot from the heat. Season to taste with salt and pepper.

2. In a medium bowl, beat the eggs with a pinch of salt and a few grindings of pepper. Stir in the 2 tablespoons chopped cilantro. Heat the remaining 1 tablespoon olive oil in a medium skillet over medium heat until shimmering. Pour in the eggs and scramble until just barely set, 4 to 5 minutes.

3. Spoon the eggs into the sauce and stir to incorporate. Add the tortilla chips and gently stir to coat in the sauce. Don't worry if the chips break a bit.

4. Spoon the chilaquiles into bowls. Generously dollop the green chile sauce over the chilaquiles. Scatter the avocado on top, drizzle with the crema, garnish with more cilantro, and serve.

potato– parsnip hash–kes

Having been raised in the Deep South, I grew up eating hash browns. When I moved to New York, I tried my first latke at Barney Greengrass deli. I was immediately enamored with the crunchiness of this perfect mound of fried potato. Listen, I still love my mom's version of hash browns (which I later learned were just frozen shredded potatoes, fried in a pan), but I came to adore the magic that adding flour and egg creates in the traditional latke. This dish is a perfect marriage of latke and hash brown, with parsnips and garlicky sour cream performing the wedding ceremony. ~Julie

GARLICKY SOUR CREAM
4 tablespoons **olive oil**
8 **garlic cloves**, minced
¾ cup **sour cream**
Kosher salt

HASH-KES
1 large or 2 medium **parsnips**, peeled
2 large **russet potatoes**, peeled
3 tablespoons **all-purpose flour**

2 teaspoons **onion powder**
1½ teaspoons **dried dill**
½ teaspoon **kosher salt**, plus more as needed
Freshly ground black pepper
2 large **eggs**, lightly beaten
Grapeseed or **canola oil**
Chopped **fresh chives**

1. **Make the sour cream:** Heat the olive oil in a small skillet over medium heat until shimmering. Add the garlic and cook until fragrant and lightly browned, about 2 minutes. Remove from the heat and allow the garlic oil to cool for about 5 minutes, then whisk the garlic oil into the sour cream and season to taste with salt.

2. **Make the hash-kes:** Shred the parsnips with the grating disk of a food processor or grate on the large holes of a box grater. Transfer to a large bowl.

3. Next, shred the potatoes in the food processor or grate on the large holes of a box grater. Working in small batches, wrap the shredded potato in

a double layer of cheesecloth or a clean dish towel and squeeze out all the water until the potatoes are dry. Add the potatoes to the bowl with the parsnips. Your potatoes might turn gray or brown ('cuz that's what happens when starchy potatoes are exposed to oxygen), but don't sweat it— it won't affect the quality of the potatoes or latkes.

4. In a small bowl, stir together the flour, onion powder, dill, ½ teaspoon salt, and the pepper. Add to the shredded potatoes and parsnips along with the eggs and toss well to combine.

5. Heat ½ inch of the oil in a large cast-iron skillet over medium-high heat until very

hot and shimmering, but not smoking. Working in batches, shape the potato mixture into loose 3-inch discs, using a scant ¼ cup for each disc, and fry in the hot oil until golden brown and crisp on one side, 3 to 4 minutes. Carefully flip the discs and cook on the other side until crisp and brown, 3 to 4 minutes more. Use a slotted spatula to transfer to a paper towel–lined plate to drain. Sprinkle with more salt. Repeat with the remaining potato mixture, adding more oil to the skillet as needed. Dollop each little cake with garlicky sour cream, sprinkle the tops with chopped chives, and serve warm.

ain't nobody here but us chickens

This chapter is for the birds and for those who love the birds! Chicken is far and away the most popular and most requested protein in our households. There's a cut for everyone in this chapter: whole birds, spatchcocked birds, white meat, dark meat, boneless, *and* crispy skin. This chapter has some of our favorite go-to recipes for those days we are looking for a lean and healthy meal, but it also has a vast array of decadent delights for those times we want to be a little naughty! Don't forget who created these recipes: a New Mexican food enthusiast and a buttermilk junkie from Alabama.

winner, winner, chicken dinner

fried chicken

WITH CRYSTAL
HOT HONEY

You are going to have to excuse me for a moment while I lose my mind over Crystal Hot Sauce (which is pronounced creeeeee-stuhl where I'm from). This Louisiana hot sauce is rooted deep in my childhood nostalgia. With its smooth texture, medium heat level, and salty-vinegary tang, Crystal Hot Sauce also happens to make one helluva brine for chicken.

When I fry chicken for my friends and family, I love using boneless thighs. It saves everyone the trauma of witnessing me gnaw on bones. Boneless thighs also make it easier to sandwich the chicken between halves of a biscuit or a hamburger bun. ~Julie

MARINADE
4 cups **water**
¼ cup **Crystal Hot Sauce**
¼ cup **kosher salt**
2 tablespoons **sugar**

CHICKEN
6 boneless, skinless **chicken thighs**
1 cup **buttermilk**
3 tablespoons **Crystal Hot Sauce**
2½ teaspoons **kosher salt**
2 teaspoons finely grated **lemon zest**
2 teaspoons **fresh lemon juice**

1½ cups **all-purpose flour**
1 teaspoon **garlic powder**
¾ teaspoon **smoked paprika**
½ teaspoon **freshly ground black pepper**
¼ teaspoon **cayenne pepper**
Grapeseed or **canola oil**

CRYSTAL HOT HONEY
⅓ cup **honey**
1 tablespoon **Crystal Hot Sauce**

1. **Make the marinade:** In a medium saucepan, combine the water, hot sauce, salt, and sugar. Bring to a simmer over medium-high heat, stirring until the salt and sugar dissolve completely. Transfer to the freezer for about 30 minutes to cool.

2. **Make the chicken:** Place the chicken thighs in a large bowl and pour in the marinade. Cover the bowl with plastic wrap and refrigerate for at least 1 hour and up to 12 hours.

3. In a shallow dish or pie pan, whisk together the buttermilk, hot sauce, 1½ teaspoons salt, and the lemon zest and juice. In a separate shallow dish, whisk together the flour, garlic powder, paprika, pepper, cayenne, and remaining 1 teaspoon of salt.

4. Working one at a time, remove the chicken thighs from the brine, letting any excess drip back into the bowl. Coat the thighs in the buttermilk mixture, then place them in the flour and coat them to create a slightly wet, shaggy coating. Gently shake off any excess flour and transfer the chicken to a plate.

5. Heat 1 inch of the oil in a large, heavy-bottomed pot or Dutch oven over medium heat until it reaches 350°F on a deep-fry thermometer, or until a fleck of flour sizzles on contact with the oil. Working in batches to avoid overcrowding the pot, fry the chicken in the hot oil, flipping a couple of times, until deep golden brown and the internal temperature reaches at least 165°F, about 6 minutes. Transfer the chicken to a paper towel–lined plate to drain as you fry the remaining pieces. Let the oil temperature return to 350°F between batches.

6. **Make the honey sauce:** In a small bowl, whisk together the honey and hot sauce.

7. Drizzle the honey sauce over the fried chicken and serve hot or cold!

grilled chicken & romaine

This cookbook wouldn't be complete without a recipe for Alabama's white barbecue sauce. That was a no-brainer. The tricky part was deciding where it would appear, because this tangy, peppery sauce is delicious with just about anything. We wanted to showcase our version of my hometown staple in a big way, so we use it here as both a marinade and a dressing. Once you've tasted it, you may consider using it to bathe in as well.

There are countless interpretations of this white sauce, and I can just hear my Southern friends asking, "How do you do yours, Julie Beth?" Well, as a purist, I don't stray too far from the original. You know the classic saying, "If the Alabama white BBQ sauce ain't broke, why fix it?" I was raised on this sauce, and for those of you who are new to it, I am so excited for y'all to make its acquaintance. ~ Julie

4 boneless, skinless **chicken breasts** (5 to 7 ounces each)

½ cup **Alabama White BBQ Sauce** (recipe follows), plus more for serving

Grapeseed or **canola oil**, for greasing

2 heads of **romaine lettuce**, halved lengthwise

Olive oil

Kosher salt and **freshly ground black pepper**

1. Add the chicken to a large zippered plastic bag with ½ cup of the white sauce. Seal the bag and massage the sauce into the chicken. Let marinate at room temperature for 30 minutes or in the refrigerator for up to 4 hours. Reserve the remaining sauce (¾ cup) for serving.

2. Thirty minutes prior to grilling, remove the chicken from the refrigerator to let it come to room temperature. Heat a grill or a grill pan to medium heat and oil the grates well by dipping a paper towel in oil, folding it up, and using tongs to hold it, rubbing it all over the grates.

3. Brush the cut sides of the romaine with olive oil and season with salt and pepper.

4. Remove the chicken from the marinade and gently shake to allow most of the sauce to drip off. Season the chicken on both sides with salt and pepper. Cook on the grill until well browned on one side, 8 to 10 minutes. Flip the chicken breasts over and continue to cook on the other side for another 10 minutes, or until the internal temperature registers 165°F on an instant-read thermometer. Meanwhile, add the romaine to the grill and cook for 5 to 10 minutes.

5. Remove the chicken from the grill and transfer to a platter to rest while the romaine continues to cook, about 5 minutes more or until it is wilted slightly and dark grill marks form. Transfer to the platter with the chicken. Drizzle the remaining white sauce over everything and serve immediately.

alabama white bbq sauce

MAKES 1¼ CUPS

1 cup **mayonnaise**

¼ cup **apple cider vinegar**

1 teaspoon **Worcestershire sauce**

1½ teaspoons **freshly ground black pepper**

1 teaspoon **dried oregano**

½ teaspoon **celery salt**

¼ teaspoon **garlic powder**

½ teaspoon **kosher salt**

½ teaspoon **cayenne pepper** (optional)

In a medium bowl, whisk together the mayonnaise, vinegar, Worcestershire sauce, pepper, oregano, celery salt, garlic powder, salt, and cayenne, if using, until thoroughly combined.

tarragon chicken

Yes, boneless, skinless chicken breast is about as exciting as waiting in line at the post office or listening to your friends describe their dreams. Figuring out how to spruce up this white meat can be as challenging as folding a fitted sheet, so we are thrilled to present this one-pan wonder! This dish not only is a breeze to make, but it's also incredibly delicious and packs an impressive flavor profile: green, liquorice-y tarragon with the salty pop of capers. You will only need ½ cup of white wine to deglaze the pan and make the sauce, so we recommend opening a good bottle and drinking the rest of it with dinner. OMG, look at us suggesting wine pairings! ~ **J&J**

2 tablespoons **dried tarragon**

Finely grated zest of 1 **lemon**

4 boneless, skinless **chicken breasts** (about 1 pound), pounded to about ½-inch thickness

Kosher salt and **freshly ground black pepper**

2 tablespoons **olive oil**, plus more as needed

1 medium **shallot**, finely chopped

¼ cup **capers**, drained

½ cup **dry white wine**

2 tablespoons **unsalted butter**

1. In a small bowl, stir together the tarragon and the lemon zest. Season the pounded chicken breasts on both sides with salt and pepper, then rub with the tarragon mixture.

2. Heat 1 tablespoon of the olive oil in a large sauté pan or skillet over medium-high heat until hot and shimmering. Working in batches if needed, add the chicken breasts to the pan and cook until golden brown and cooked through, 3 to 4 minutes per side. Transfer the chicken to a serving platter.

3. Add the remaining tablespoon oil to the pan, then add the shallot and capers. Cook, stirring, until the capers are soft, about 3 minutes. Pour in the wine and simmer for 1 minute, scraping up any brown bits stuck to the bottom of the pan, until reduced slightly. Remove the pan from the heat and stir in the butter until melted and the sauce is emulsified (that means it looks creamy, not oily). Season to taste with salt and pepper. Pour the sauce over the chicken and serve immediately.

deglazing

"What's deglazing? That sounds fancy!" Deglazing just involves adding liquid to a hot pan to loosen and pull up those delicious bits of charred food that stick to the bottom. It creates an insanely delicious sauce while also giving you a head start at cleaning your pan afterward. We use wine here, but you can also use chicken, beef, or vegetable broth or something acidic, like red wine vinegar or lemon juice.

chicken & dumplings

When I am feeling stressed, I have my go-to comfort foods: ice cream, pizza, and boxed wine. (It's a food!) For Julie, it was always chicken and dumplings, which to her surprise I had never made before. I wanted to try my hand at it during the stressful spring of 2020. Because certain ingredients were hard to find during that time, I had to make several substitutions and alterations to her tried-and-true recipe. By the time I finished, I had completely changed her dish—to amazingly great results. So, even though Julie is the master chicken-and-dumplings creator in this relationship, we offer you my version here as a reminder that cooking should never be taken too seriously. Listen, if it doesn't work out, you still have the pizza and boxed wine to carry you through the rough times—but if you need a surefire win, this chicken and dumplings is your answer. ~ Jesse

CHICKEN

- 2 pounds boneless, skinless **chicken thighs** or **breasts**
- 1 teaspoon **black peppercorns**
- 1 **dried bay leaf**
- 5 cups **chicken broth**
- 3 tablespoons **unsalted butter**
- 2 medium **sweet potatoes**, peeled and cut into ½-inch dice
- 1 medium **onion**, chopped
- ½ cup chopped **fennel bulb**
- 2 **garlic cloves**, minced
- **Kosher salt** and **freshly ground black pepper**
- ¼ cup **all-purpose flour**
- 1 cup fresh or frozen **peas**
- 1 cup bite-size **broccoli florets**

DUMPLINGS

- 1⅔ cups **all-purpose flour**
- 1½ teaspoons **kosher salt**
- ½ teaspoon **freshly ground black pepper**
- 2 teaspoons **baking powder**
- 2 teaspoons chopped **fresh thyme**
- 1 tablespoon chopped **fresh parsley**, plus more for garnish
- 4 tablespoons (½ stick) **unsalted butter**, cut into dice and chilled in freezer for at least 20 minutes
- ¾ cup **whole milk**

1. Make the chicken: Add the chicken, peppercorns, bay leaf, and broth to a large, deep pot. Bring to a simmer over medium-high heat, then reduce the heat to medium low and gently simmer until the chicken is tender, 40 to 45 minutes. Transfer the chicken to a plate to cool. Strain the stock through a fine-mesh sieve into a large bowl and discard the solids. You'll need about 4 cups of broth. Once the chicken has cooled, shred the meat. You should have about 3 cups of shredded chicken.

2. Wipe out the pot, then melt the butter over medium-high heat. Add the sweet potatoes, onion, and fennel and cook until the vegetables are softened but not completely tender, 3 to 4 minutes. Add the garlic and cook until fragrant, about 1 minute. Season with a big pinch of salt and pepper. Sprinkle in the flour and cook, stirring and scraping the bottom of the pot, until the vegetables are well coated and the flour starts to toast, 1 to 2 minutes.

recipe continues . . .

3. Gradually pour in the reserved 4 cups of broth. Bring to a boil, then reduce the heat to medium. Stir in the shredded chicken, the peas, and broccoli and simmer until the peas and broccoli are tender and the chicken is warmed through, 5 to 7 minutes. Season to taste with more salt and pepper. Reduce the heat to medium low and cover.

1. Make the dumplings: In a large bowl, whisk together the flour, salt, pepper, baking powder, thyme, and parsley. Add the butter and use your fingertips to work it into the flour until broken down into pea-size pieces. Add the milk and stir with a fork until the dough just comes together. Shape the dough into 8 to 10 gently packed 2- to 3-inch balls, being careful not to overwork.

5. Uncover the stew and increase the heat to medium. Once the liquid is again simmering, gently drop in the dough balls, cover the pot, and simmer until the dumplings are cooked through, 15 to 20 minutes.

6. Ladle the chicken and dumplings into bowls, garnish with more chopped parsley, and serve hot.

winner, winner, chicken dinner

BUTTERMILK ROASTED CHICKEN WITH CRUNCHY CROUTONS

My mom's recipe for a roast chicken was as simple as this: butter, salt, pepper. If she was feeling extra fancy, she would season the chicken with Dale's Steak Seasoning, the self-proclaimed #1 Marinade in the Nation, manufactured and bottled right in Alabama! As I got older, I discovered there are more flavorful (and less sodium-forward) approaches. Soaking the chicken in buttermilk for at least 6 hours is one of the simplest (but not quickest) ways to elevate a roasted bird. Not only do you get great acidity and tenderness from the buttermilk, but it also helps the chicken brown and crisp. Everybody will be fighting over the crispy skin, as well as clamoring for the treasure trove of croutons that have been sitting beneath the chicken, soaking up all those delicious juices. As a tribute to my mom, this recipe still includes salt and pepper—but no Dale's. ~ Julie

2 cups **buttermilk**

3 tablespoons **kosher salt**

4 sprigs of **fresh rosemary**

1 (3½- to 4-pound) **whole roasting chicken**

1 tablespoon **grapeseed** or **canola oil**

1 **lemon**, sliced into 4 wedges

8 **garlic cloves**, smashed

1 (10-ounce) **baguette**

4 tablespoons (½ stick) **unsalted butter**, melted

1 teaspoon **freshly ground black pepper**

1. Combine the buttermilk, 2 tablespoons of the salt, and 1 sprig of rosemary in a gallon-size zippered plastic bag and shake to distribute the salt. Add the chicken, seal the bag, and gently shake and massage to fully coat the chicken. Marinate breast side down in the refrigerator for at least 6 hours, or overnight. About 1 hour before roasting, remove the chicken from the refrigerator and let it come to room temperature.

2. Preheat the oven to 425°F. Pour the oil into a large cast-iron skillet. Place the skillet in the oven for 10 minutes to preheat.

3. Remove the chicken from the buttermilk, letting as much marinade as possible drip back into the bag. Discard the bag and marinade. Pat the chicken dry with paper towels. Stuff the chicken cavity with the lemon wedges, 4 of the garlic cloves, and 1 sprig of rosemary. Tie the chicken legs together at the tips with twine to close tightly. (Put that chicken on house arrest!)

4. Cut or tear the baguette into 1-inch cubes. Carefully remove the hot skillet from the oven and spread the bread cubes on the bottom in a single

recipe continues . . .

layer. Top with the remaining 2 sprigs of rosemary and nestle the remaining 4 garlic cloves among the bread cubes. Brush the chicken all over with the melted butter, making sure to get all sides, between the thighs, and in all the crevices. Season the chicken all over with the remaining tablespoon of salt and the pepper. Place the chicken breast side up on top of the bread cubes. Tuck the wing tips under the body.

5. Roast the chicken for 20 minutes. Reduce the oven temperature to 375°F and continue roasting for 60 to 70 minutes more, tenting with foil if the skin is getting too dark, until the croutons are golden brown and an instant-read thermometer inserted into the breast registers 150°F and the thighs and legs register at least 165°F. Remove the chicken from the oven and let rest in the pan for 15 minutes. Carve the chicken directly over the croutons and let those juices flow, honey! Serve with the croutons.

SERVES
4

chicken & asparagus sheet pan dinner

The old-school stoves like the one my parents had when I was growing up had their broilers in a drawer under the oven. Ours remained mostly untouched because it served as a graveyard for weird, sticky pans, rarely used muffin tins, and strangely, once, my retainer. Recently, though, I've discovered the joys of the broiler, which allows you to cook food directly under the heat source. I use it for anything else that will benefit from a browned, caramelized finish. This dinner allows you to use your broiler in a way that you can walk away from the oven, walk back, flip things over, and Poof! You have a delectable, crispy-topped dinner.

The beauty of a good marinade is that it is a building block for so many taste combinations. This creamy coconut marinade, gently sweetened with honey and seasoned with ginger and soy sauce, is incredibly versatile. Not in the mood for chicken? Substitute shrimp, veggies, or sirloin. If I am ever on a cooking competition show, this will be the marinade "I've made a thousand times and know like the back of my hand"—although, when people say that, they always end up getting eliminated. But don't worry, because this dinner is a guaranteed win! ~ Jesse

2 pounds boneless, skinless **chicken thighs**

1 teaspoon **kosher salt**, plus more as needed

½ teaspoon **freshly ground black pepper**

2 tablespoons **soy sauce**

2 tablespoons **fish sauce**

3 tablespoons **honey**

3 **garlic cloves**, minced

½ tablespoon minced **fresh ginger**

Juice of ½ **orange**

2 teaspoons **toasted sesame oil**

1 tablespoon refined **peanut oil**

Finely grated zest and juice of 1 **lime**

3 tablespoons canned **full-fat coconut milk**

1 tablespoon **cornstarch**

Nonstick cooking spray

1 pound **asparagus**, tough ends trimmed, spears cut in half

Cooked rice of choice, warmed

Sesame seeds

Fresh cilantro leaves

1. Pat the chicken thighs dry with paper towels and cut into 1½- to 2-inch pieces. Season with the 1 teaspoon salt and ½ teaspoon pepper.

2. In a large bowl, whisk together the soy sauce, fish sauce, honey, garlic, ginger, orange juice, sesame oil, peanut oil, lime zest and juice, coconut milk, and cornstarch. Add the chicken and toss to coat. Let marinate at room temperature for 20 to 30 minutes, or in the refrigerator at least 2 hours and up to overnight.

3. Preheat the broiler and arrange a rack in the upper third of the oven. Lightly grease a large sheet pan or rimmed baking sheet with nonstick cooking spray.

4. Using a slotted spoon, scoop the chicken from the marinade and arrange on one side of the sheet pan in a single layer. Place the asparagus on the other side of the pan and season with some salt and pepper. Pour the marinade over everything. Broil, stirring halfway through, until the chicken is cooked through, the asparagus is nicely browned, and the sauce has thickened slightly, 10 to 12 minutes. Serve over rice and garnish with the sesame seeds and cilantro.

green chile chicken enchilada pie

SERVES
6

Green chile chicken enchiladas are far and away *the* defining dish of my childhood. My mom would make hers as a casserole, serving it cut into big squares. Rolling up the stuffed tortillas individually was just too much work for her and it was easier to layer all the ingredients in a pan, place the pan in the oven to bake, and walk away. If there is ever a green chile chicken enchilada dish on a restaurant menu, you can bet your bottom dollar I am going to order it.

On our last day during a vacation in San Francisco, Justin and I discovered a place that made green chile and chicken potpies—and it was closed! I couldn't stop thinking about it, though. I hadn't even tasted this pie, and it was controlling my life. When I returned home, I decided to concoct my own version. This was during my "piecrust is the devil" phase, so the end result was a bit of a disaster. It took me a few years before I thought to abandon the traditional piecrust and use corn tortillas to make the "crust." After all, the tortillas are my favorite part of an enchilada. The filling here, made with a roux and packed with peas, carrots, and onion, keeps this dish firmly in the potpie category, while the green chile sauce and corn tortilla crust allow it to live its life as an enchilada, too. No restrictive labels here! Celebrate diversity and individuality! Do your thing, Green Chile Chicken Enchilada Pie! ~Jesse

2 tablespoons **unsalted butter**

1 small **onion**, diced

1 medium **carrot**, cut into ⅓-inch dice

2 teaspoons **dried oregano**

¼ teaspoon **ground cumin**

1 teaspoon **kosher salt**, plus more as needed

½ teaspoon **freshly ground black pepper**, plus more as needed

¼ cup **all-purpose flour**

1⅓ cups **chicken broth**

¼ cup **whole milk**

½ cup **frozen peas**

1 (4-ounce) can diced **Hatch green chiles**

1 cup diced **cooked chicken** (from 1 large breast or a couple of thighs)

2 cups shredded **cheddar** and **Monterey jack cheese**

8 (6-inch) **corn tortillas**

2 tablespoons **canola oil**

1 cup Hatch Green Chile Sauce (page 64), plus more for serving

Sour cream

1. Melt the butter in a large saucepan over medium heat. Add the onion, carrots, oregano, cumin, 1 teaspoon salt, and ½ teaspoon pepper and cook until the onion is translucent and the carrots are softened, about 5 minutes. Add the flour and stir until the vegetables are well coated and the flour is toasted, 2 to 3 minutes. Slowly pour in the broth, whisking constantly to prevent lumps from forming. Whisk in the milk. Simmer for about 5 minutes, whisking frequently, until thickened.

2. Stir in the frozen peas, green chiles, and chicken. Cook until warmed through, 3 minutes. Turn off the heat and stir in 1 cup of the cheese until melted. Season to taste with more salt and pepper. Cover to keep warm while you prepare the crust.

recipe continues . . .

3. Preheat the broiler.

4. Cut 6 of the tortillas in half. Heat the oil in a medium skillet over medium-high heat until nearly smoking. Add the whole and halved tortillas, a few at a time, and cook until they're starting to bubble and crisp but are still pliable, 5 to 10 seconds on each side. Transfer to a paper towel–lined plate to drain and cool.

5. Place a whole fried tortilla in the center of a 9-inch pie pan. Arrange 6 tortilla halves, curved side up, around the sides of the dish, slightly overlapping each other and the center tortilla. Sprinkle ½ cup of the shredded cheese over the tortilla crust. Broil for 1 to 2 minutes, until the cheese is melted, bubbling, and starting to brown.

6. Arrange the remaining halved tortillas, curved side up, around the edge of the pie dish, slightly overlapping the lower ring of tortillas. Spread the filling over the cheesy tortilla crust, then fold the outer ring of tortillas toward the center and place the remaining whole tortilla in the center, encasing the filling. Evenly spread the 1 cup chile sauce over the tortillas. Sprinkle the remaining ½ cup shredded cheese on top. Broil until the cheese on top is browned and bubbling, 2 to 3 minutes.

7. Let the enchilada pie stand for 10 minutes, then slice and serve with sour cream and more green chile sauce alongside.

CHILE
WITH AN E
~BY JESSE

There are gateway drugs and there are gateway ingredients. This is a cookbook, so I trust you can imagine which kind I'm going to address here. Chile is my gateway ingredient. Let me back up for a moment.

As a redhead with a tendency for heartburn, I don't think it's genetically natural for me to love spicy food as much as I do. My alabaster skin turns pink and ruddy, my eyes water, and sweat beads out of every pore of my body. If there is a case for nurture over nature, my love for heat is definitely it. (That's heat in terms of spice, not weather; you'll find me in the shade complaining about the humidity until the day I die.)

My passion for chile was conceived in my hometown of Albuquerque, New Mexico, where Hatch green chiles are more popular than *Breaking Bad,* and red chile sauce runs like the New Mexican version of the Seine— so I guess that would be the Rio Grande River. These flavors were not only present on our kitchen table at home but were also wildly available at almost every restaurant in town. The question "Red or green?" was our "Salad or fries?"

Hatch green chiles are actually named after the region from which they are harvested. Every year during Labor Day weekend, the tiny town of Hatch, New Mexico (population 1,680), welcomes more than 30,000 people for its annual Hatch Chile Festival. The Hatch Valley also produces a red chile (commonly found in grocery stores, labeled as "New Mexico Chile"), and I became transfixed by the subtle differences among the array of chiles I was exposed to during these years. I was introduced to Mexican varieties: bright and mild guajillos and fruity, smoky anchos. I learned that the smaller pods, like chiles de árbol or pequín, packed much more heat in their tiny frames. I met super-mild California varieties from the Anaheim region. If it was a chile, I was interested not only in getting to know it but also in getting to know all about it—where it came from, how it was harvested, how it could be used in the kitchen.

Early on, I worked at a popular local restaurant called Sadie's Cocina, where I learned just how nuanced chiles could be. Sampling various batches of enchilada sauce or salsa taught me how subtly different the chiles could taste, based on something as simple as the weather that season. Those details fascinated me.

As a teenager, after I moved to New York City for acting school, I would still make Sadie's Cocina my first stop when I went home for the holidays. Green chile chicken enchiladas with a side of their homemade chips and salsa is still my favorite meal to come home to. I just pop a Pepcid for dessert.

Living in New York in those years, I craved the flavors that were indigenous to New Mexico. I was pushed to find new kinds of heat and, in turn, my palate was opened to a world of spices beyond my home. My taste buds were taken to countries the rest of me hadn't ever traveled to. I encountered the tangy, bright curries of India, the numbing Sichuan peppercorns of China, and the "fool me twice, shame on me" kick of wasabi from Japan. (I thought it was avocado the first time I came upon it . . . and the second time as well.)

I began a torrid love affair with all these new seasonings, these new forms of heat. I had no idea when I fell in love with the beauty of a roasted Hatch green chile at the age of eight that this wider world of flavors even existed, but I am so happy to be aware of these possibilities now. And lucky for me, I get to publish a few of them in this book! I hope you enjoy them, too!

But now, I bring you back to my origins with these two staples. The red and green chile sauces are the contrasting building blocks of New Mexican cuisine. As with any chile sauce, there are grace notes and nuances. No two batches will ever taste exactly the same, because some chiles will inevitably be hotter than others.

Introducing you to these two sauces sort of feels like bringing home a new boyfriend for Christmas. I love them so much and I can't wait for you to meet them. Also, I really don't want you to embarrass me in front of them.

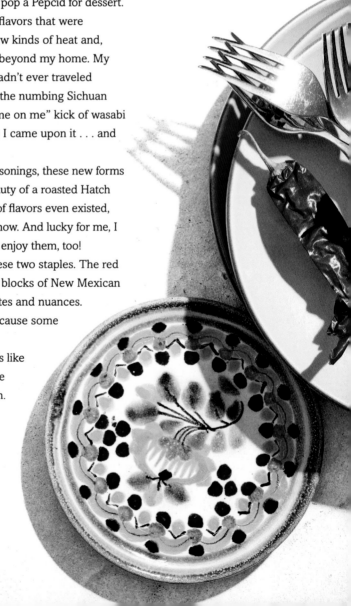

hatch green chile sauce

Tangy and bright, this green chile sauce is incredibly versatile. It is a major player in our enchilada pie (see page 59) and as a final punch in our Christmas Chilaquiles (page 41) or in the scrambled eggs for stuffed sopaipillas (see page 108). ~Jesse

1 tablespoon **olive oil**

1 small **white onion**, diced

1 **jalapeño**, seeded and diced

4 **garlic cloves**, smashed and roughly chopped

1½ teaspoons **ground cumin**

1 teaspoon **kosher salt**, plus more as needed

½ teaspoon **freshly ground black pepper**, plus more as needed

1 cup **chicken** or **vegetable broth**

3 (4-ounce) cans diced **Hatch green chiles**

1. Heat the olive oil in a medium saucepan over medium heat. When the oil is shimmering, add the onion and jalapeño and sauté until soft and translucent but not browned, 4 to 5 minutes. Add the garlic, cumin, 1 teaspoon salt, and ½ teaspoon pepper and cook until fragrant, 1 to 2 minutes. Add the broth and green chiles and stir to scrape up any stuck bits from the bottom of the pan.

2. Carefully transfer the mixture to a food processor or high-speed blender and puree until completely smooth. Season to taste with more salt and pepper. Use immediately or transfer to an airtight container. (Sauce can be stored in the refrigerator for up to 4 days or in the freezer up to 3 months. I like to freeze small batches in ice cube trays or zippered plastic bags.)

new mexican red chile sauce

Full-bodied and robust, red chiles create the merlot of sauces. Capable of contributing to so much more than just enchiladas, this sauce can add deep smoky richness to braised chicken and work in perfect tandem with its BFF, Hatch Green Chile Sauce (page 64), as in the Christmas Chilaquiles (page 41). After one batch of this, you will swear off ever buying the canned stuff again. Dried whole chiles are available in most supermarkets, usually in the produce section. There are several varieties to choose from, but I recommend reaching for the guajillos with their sweet, earthy flavor and medium heat, or the anchos, which are a milder variety with fruity smokiness. If you happen to find New Mexico chiles, by all means grab 'em! With their slightly darker color, they create an earthy and robust sauce with a hint of sage and cherry. If you find yourself torn about which variety to choose, I say be brave: grab a couple of varieties and combine! ~Jesse

- 3 ounces **dried chiles**, such as guajillo, ancho, and/or New Mexico
- ½ medium **onion**, root end trimmed, then quartered
- 3 **garlic cloves**
- 2 ripe **Roma (plum) tomatoes**
- 3 cups **chicken** or **vegetable broth**
- 1½ teaspoons **kosher salt**, plus more as needed
- 2 tablespoons **honey**, plus more as needed
- 1 teaspoon **dried Mexican oregano** (see Note, page 140)
- 1 teaspoon **ground cumin**

handy hint

Protect those hands! I highly recommend using a pair of latex gloves while working with chiles. If you don't have a pair, just make sure you wash your hands really, really well after handling the chiles—and for God's sake, don't rub your eyes.

1. Preheat the oven to 350°F. Line a baking sheet with foil.

2. Use a pair of kitchen shears to snip the stems off the chiles. Cut in half lengthwise and brush out most of the seeds and any large veins. Lay the chiles on the baking sheet and toast in the oven for 3 minutes, until fragrant and darkened a shade. Transfer the chiles to a medium saucepan with a lid.

3. Arrange the onion, garlic, and tomato on the same baking sheet. Roast for 20 minutes, until softened and starting to lightly char in spots.

4. Meanwhile, add the broth to the saucepan with the chiles and bring to a simmer over medium-high heat. Cover and turn off the heat. Let the chiles soften in the warm broth while the vegetables continue roasting.

5. Add the roasted onion, garlic, and tomato to a blender or food processor, along with 1½ teaspoons salt, 2 tablespoons honey, the oregano, and cumin. Carefully pour in the chiles and their soaking liquid. Blend on high speed until smooth. Season to taste with more salt or honey. Use immediately or transfer to an airtight container. (Sauce can be stored in the refrigerator for up to 1 week or in the freezer for up to 3 months.)

braised chicken thighs

SERVES
4

WITH VIDALIA
ONIONS &
CABBAGE

Chicken thighs are far and away my favorite chicken cut. Full of rich flavor and possibility, they allow you to do just about anything with them. No method is easier or more foolproof than braising. Here, we sear the thighs first to give the skin a head start, before tucking it in with sweet Vidalia onions and cabbage to braise in these delicious juices.

A good spice blend is a valuable item in the pantry arsenal, but I'm too much of a micromanager to go with commercial varieties. I like to create my own, so let me introduce 'Que Dust. Whether as a dry rub or as a finishing seasoning, it's great in so many applications. We've incorporated it into the Fennel-Rubbed Spare Ribs (page 97), but don't stop there! Sprinkle it on corn, potatoes, any veggie before roasting or grilling—the sky's the limit. (And the sky is really high, although I do think it technically ends once you reach outer space.) ~ Jesse

6 to 8 bone-in, skin-on **chicken thighs** (about 3 pounds)
Kosher salt
Freshly ground black pepper
2 to 3 tablespoons **grapeseed** or **canola oil**
½ medium head of **green cabbage**, core removed, sliced crosswise into ¼-inch strips

1 large **Vidalia** or other **sweet onion**, cut in half and sliced into ¼-inch half-moons
1 medium **shallot**, cut in half and sliced into ¼-inch half-moons
2 **dried bay leaves**
5 **garlic cloves**, minced
2 tablespoons **'Que Dust** (recipe follows)
1¾ cups **chicken broth**
3 tablespoons **apple cider vinegar**

1. Let the chicken thighs sit at room temperature for 30 minutes. Pat dry with paper towels and season with salt and pepper.

2. Preheat the oven to 350°F.

3. Heat the oil in a large ovenproof skillet with high sides over medium-high heat until shimmering. Add the chicken, skin-side down, and cook without disturbing until well browned, 6 to 8 minutes (reduce the heat to medium if the pan starts smoking). Flip the chicken and brown on the other side for about 1 minute. Transfer to a plate.

4. Add the cabbage, onion, shallot, and bay leaves to the pan. Season with salt and pepper and cook until everything has turned golden brown, 7 to 8 minutes. Stir in the garlic and 'Que Dust and cook until fragrant, 1 minute. Add the broth and vinegar, stirring to scrape up browned bits from the bottom of the pan. Bring to a simmer and cook for 3 to 4 minutes. Season with more salt and pepper.

5. Nestle the chicken thighs, skin side up, in the pan again, partially submerging them in the braising liquid but keeping the skin exposed. Transfer to the oven and bake until the skin is golden brown and the liquid has reduced slightly, 45 minutes. Let the chicken rest 10 minutes before serving.

'que dust

MAKES ABOUT ¾ CUP

¼ cup **paprika**

2 tablespoons **kosher salt**

2½ tablespoons **sugar**

1 tablespoon **dry mustard**

2 tablespoons **ancho chile powder** or **chili powder**

1 tablespoon **ground cumin**

1 tablespoon **freshly ground black pepper**

½ tablespoon **Hatch green chile powder** or **cayenne pepper**

In a small resealable container, combine the paprika, salt, sugar, mustard, ancho chile powder, cumin, pepper, and Hatch chile powder. Cover and shake well to blend. (The dry spice mix will keep at room temperature up to 1 year.)

sorghum butter spatchcocked chicken

WITH
PARSNIPS

Spatchcock! The word will never *not* make me giggle. It sounds like something that would happen at a wedding on *Game of Thrones*. But spatchcocking is simply the process of flattening a bird by splitting it and removing the backbone. (Actually, I think this *was* on an episode of *Game of Thrones*.) Not only does this process allow the chicken to cook faster, but it also exposes more skin to crisp up. We give our bird a nice sorghum-butter massage that brings a rich, sweet-savory complexity to the meat.

Roasting a chicken without adding something else to the pan is like visiting Disneyland and only going to the Hall of Presidents. What's the point? The juices from a roasting chicken are liquid gold. We are obsessed with the parsnips here, but there are really very few limits to what you could use: carrots, Brussels, thick chunks of sourdough—the list goes on and on. ~ **Julie**

1 (3½- to 4-pound) **roasting chicken**, spatchcocked (see Note)

4 tablespoons **Sorghum Butter** (page 263)

1 teaspoon **kosher salt**, plus more as needed

Freshly ground black pepper

3 or 4 **parsnips** (about 1 pound), peeled and cut into 2- to 3-inch pieces

3 or 4 sprigs of **fresh thyme**

Olive oil

Juice of ½ **lemon**

Crusty French bread

note

You can ask a butcher to spatchcock the chicken, but it's not hard to do it yourself. Get some heavy-duty kitchen shears, and lay the bird breast side down with the legs pointing toward you. Starting at the cavity, cut up both sides along the backbone to the neck. Pull up and remove the backbone. Then flip the chicken and place on a flat surface. Press down firmly so the chicken lies flat.

1. Pat the chicken dry with paper towels and allow to sit at room temperature for 30 minutes.

2. Preheat the oven to 400°F. Arrange a rack in the center of the oven.

3. Pat the chicken dry again, then rub the sorghum butter all over the top and underside of the chicken. Use your fingers to gently separate the skin from the meat and smear the butter underneath the skin, massaging to get it as evenly coated as possible. Arrange the skin back into place. Season all over with the 1 teaspoon salt and some pepper.

4. Scatter the parsnips and thyme sprigs in the bottom of a large cast-iron skillet or roasting pan. Drizzle with a little olive oil and season with more salt and pepper. Place the chicken on top, tucking the wingtips under the body so they don't burn. Roast the chicken for 20 minutes, then reduce the oven temperature to 375°F and continue roasting for another 40 to 45 minutes, or until an instant-read thermometer inserted into the breast registers 150°F and the thighs and legs register at least 165°F. If the skin is beginning to burn before the chicken is done roasting, tent with a sheet of foil.

5. Remove the chicken from the oven, squeeze the lemon juice all over, and let the chicken rest for 10 minutes. Carve the chicken and serve with the parsnips, pan juices, and crusty French bread to soak up that juice.

SLOW
LIKE SORGHUM
~BY JULIE

The Deep South has a lot of reputations, and moving fast isn't one of them. Southerners are known to take their time. There's a reason people love visiting and vacationing there: to escape the crowds and noise of city living, to enjoy a slow-paced life for a minute. In college, my friends gave me the nickname "Molasses" because I was always the last one ready to go and because molasses is faster to say than "sorghum syrup." I have a profound appreciation not only for the food I grew up eating down South but also for that slow-paced life. Slow like sorghum syrup.

This complex syrup deserves our attention. Sorghum syrup is made from the green juice of the sorghum plant. It brings exciting life to baked goods and a caramel-y depth to savory dishes, like pork chops, chicken, and even root vegetables. I have experimented with molasses, maple syrup, and honey as an alternative, but none of them compares. Sorghum syrup has a buttery and slightly sour bite, and when paired with salt and butter, it achieves a depth of flavor like you wouldn't believe.

My dad was raised in Holly Pond, Alabama, or as he refers to it, "Rough Edge," which boasts a whopping population of about 800 people. James Edward and Wilma Pauline, along with their eight children (my dad was third in line), grew their own sorghum canes on their farm. My dad and his siblings would harvest the canes by hand and take them to a local mill, where the canes would be fed into a two-cylinder pressing machine that was pulled by a mule who walked in circles to turn the gears. The mill crushed the canes, squeezing out the sweet green juice, which was then cooked down and strained to create a clean, thick, and flavorful syrup. They'd take home their batch in mason jars. Dessert for my dad and his brothers was sorghum syrup and buttermilk biscuits crumbled in coffee.

I vividly remember many mornings at the breakfast table with my dad, watching him thoughtfully dip his spoon into a jar of sorghum, and just as slowly, as it fell from his spoon onto a buttered homemade biscuit, he'd tell me what seemed like a never-ending story. It was as if each word were keeping pace with the rich, amber-colored drip. It was a foreign condiment; a relic from another time—even the bottle was unmarked. I'd definitely never seen a bottle of it in any of my friends' pantries. Indeed, my friends' pantries had fun things like Smurfberry Crunch cereal and Ghostbusters Hi-C Ecto Cooler boxed drinks. In our pantry, you could find Shredded Wheat cereal and Fig Newtons cookies because, in 1979, my dad decided it was time to quit smoking, start running, and get healthy. It was an unfortunate time to be his kid. Sorghum reminds me of him, though. During the writing of this cookbook, as I shared some of my ideas with my dad, he admitted that he never knew how versatile sorghum syrup is. "I just always drizzled it on my biscuits." He seemed pleased.

Like a lot of truly special ingredients, sorghum can be a tad tricky to find. When buying it, make sure the ingredients list indicates 100% pure sorghum. Imposters will include maple syrup or other sweeteners. We used to take day trips up to Tennessee and buy the most delicious sorghum from the Amish communities there. If you happen to live in Alabama, like I did, it's as easy as visiting the nearest farmers' market. But it's also always just a few clicks away on Amazon.com.

In a time when we're all swiping our phones constantly, it's good to have things in your life that slow the pace just a bit. Forget that meditation app and buy yourself a bottle of sorghum.

garlicky sorghum chicken stir-fry

This crowd pleaser is one of our favorite ways to use sorghum syrup in a savory dish. If you read my love letter to sorghum syrup (well, did you read it? It's literally on the page before this one), you'll learn that you can use molasses in a pinch, but if you do, I don't want to know about it.

I have always loved stir-fries—they are so adaptable. This sweet-savory version incorporates broccoli, scallions, basil, and Jesse's favorite, water chestnuts; but feel free to get creative and use with whatever looks fresh and delicious. Asparagus! Sugar snap peas! Green beans! A stir-fry is really just an adult version of a sandbox—without sand—that happens to be on your stovetop. ~Julie

¼ cup **sorghum syrup** (or **molasses**)

¼ cup **soy sauce**

1 tablespoon **rice vinegar**

2 teaspoons **fish sauce**

1 tablespoon **toasted sesame oil**

2 teaspoons **sriracha**, plus more as needed

1 tablespoon **cornstarch**

5 tablespoons **peanut oil**

2 pounds boneless, skinless **chicken thighs** or **breasts**, cut into 1-inch cubes

1 medium head of **broccoli**, cut into small florets

Kosher salt and freshly ground black **pepper**

1 teaspoon grated **fresh ginger**

3 **garlic cloves**, minced

1 (8-ounce) can **water chestnuts**, drained

3 **scallions**, green and white parts, trimmed and sliced on the diagonal

Chopped toasted **cashews**

Thinly sliced fresh **basil**

Cooked white rice, warmed

1. In a small bowl, whisk together the sorghum syrup, soy sauce, vinegar, fish sauce, sesame oil, 2 teaspoons sriracha, and cornstarch until the cornstarch is dissolved.

2. Heat 3 tablespoons of peanut oil in a wok or large skillet over medium-high heat. When the oil is shimmering, add the chicken and stir-fry just until there is no visible pink remaining, 4 to 5 minutes. Add the broccoli, season with salt and pepper, and continue cooking, stirring, until tender and the chicken is cooked through, about 4 minutes more. Transfer the broccoli and chicken to a medium bowl.

3. Reduce the heat to medium. Add the remaining 2 tablespoons of peanut oil to the pan. Add the ginger and garlic and cook until fragrant, 1 minute. Pour in the sorghum sauce and cook until the sauce has thickened, another 1 to 2 minutes. Add the chicken and broccoli and any accumulated juices from the bowl, along with the water chestnuts and scallions, and toss to coat with the sauce. Cook until warmed through, 3 to 5 minutes. Garnish with the cashews and basil and serve over rice.

honey-garlic grilled chicken

WITH PICKLED CHILES & PEACHES

One of the perks of living on the West Coast is that the weather is nice enough to grill year-round, although I was raised to never let inclement weather stop me. Proof in point, I have witnessed my dad command a grill in the middle of a hailstorm. (It was similar to that scene in *The Revenant* when Leo goes head to head with the grizzly bear.) In my head, I'm just as much of a badass, but it took me a long time to master the art of grilling. My temporarily singed left eyebrow can tell you all about it someday.

Pickled chiles and sweet peaches work in harmony with the marinade here. In fact, it's a perfect summertime meal, one that I'm sure my dad would also be able to conquer in a hailstorm. ~ **Jesse**

CHICKEN

¼ cup **honey**

½ cup **olive oil**

Juice of 2 **lemons**

2 **garlic cloves**, minced

1 tablespoon **kosher salt**

1 teaspoon **freshly ground black pepper**

2 pounds boneless, skinless **chicken thighs**

Grapeseed or **canola oil**

PICKLED CHILES AND PEACHES

1 **serrano chile** or **jalapeño**, seeded and thinly sliced

¼ medium **red onion**, cut in half and thinly sliced into half-moons

1 cup **water**

½ cup **apple cider vinegar**

1 tablespoon **honey**

2 teaspoons **kosher salt**

3 ripe **peaches**, halved, pitted, and sliced

ASSEMBLY

4 cups **fresh arugula**

1 cup torn **fresh basil**

¼ cup chopped **fresh chives**

1 tablespoon **olive oil**

1. Marinate the chicken: In a small bowl, whisk together the honey, olive oil, lemon juice, garlic, salt, and pepper. Pour into a gallon-size zippered plastic bag. Add the chicken, seal the bag, and massage to coat the chicken. Marinate in the refrigerator for at least 1 hour, or let sit at room temperature for 30 minutes.

2. Make the pickled chiles and peaches: Add the serrano and onion to a heatproof medium bowl. In a small saucepan, whisk together the water, vinegar, honey,

and salt. Bring to a boil over medium-high heat. Pour the vinegar mixture over the serrano and onion. Cover the bowl with plastic wrap and let stand at room temperature for 15 minutes. Add the sliced peaches and let marinate for about 5 minutes. Strain the mixture, carefully setting aside the pickled chiles, onion, and peaches and reserving 3 tablespoons of the liquid.

3. Heat a greased grill or grill pan to medium-high. Remove the chicken from the marinade and shake gently to remove

excess marinade. Season both sides of the chicken with a little more salt and pepper. Grill the chicken until nicely browned on both sides, flipping occasionally, about 15 minutes total.

4. Assemble the salad: Place the arugula, basil, and chives in a large bowl and gently toss with the olive oil and reserved pickling liquid. Add the pickled chiles, onion, and peaches. Season with salt and pepper. Serve the grilled chicken alongside the salad.

baked chicken tenders

Superman has kryptonite and Justin has chicken tenders. He crumbles under the very thought of them—every single time. Justin in a hotel: "I wonder if they have chicken tenders on the room service menu." Justin at a pool: "Mmmmm. I just saw some chicken tenders go by." Justin to the twelve-year-girl sitting at the table next to him at a restaurant: "They say I'm too old for the children's menu; can I take a quick peek at yours?" Justin to us when we decided to write this book: "You are putting chicken tenders in the book, right?" So these tenders are for Justin. Please enjoy. ~ **J&J**

1 cup **panko bread crumbs**
½ cup **standard bread crumbs**
2½ tablespoons **sesame seeds**
3 teaspoons **kosher salt**, plus more as needed
1 tablespoon **dried minced onion**
1 teaspoon **celery seed**
1 teaspoon **garlic powder**

1½ teaspoons **paprika**
½ teaspoon **ground white pepper**
¼ teaspoon **cayenne pepper** (optional)
1 cup **all-purpose flour**
3 large **eggs**
2 pounds **chicken tenders** (or chicken breasts, pounded thin and cut into strips)
Buttermilk Ranch (recipe follows)

1. Preheat the oven to 400°F.

2. Spread the panko in an even layer on a large rimmed baking sheet or sheet pan and toast until golden brown, about 4 minutes. Watch closely, as the panko can burn quickly. Transfer the toasted panko to a shallow dish and add the standard bread crumbs, sesame seeds, 2 teaspoons salt, the dried onion, celery seed, garlic powder, paprika, white pepper, and cayenne, if using. In another shallow dish, whisk the flour with the remaining teaspoon salt. In a third shallow dish, lightly beat the eggs.

3. Increase the oven to 450°F. Set a wire rack inside the baking sheet.

4. Coat the chicken tenders first in the flour, then in the egg, then in the seasoned bread crumbs, pressing the crumbs to adhere. Place the tenders on the wire rack (you may need to bake in batches, depending on the size of the rack). Bake until golden brown and cooked through, 12 to 15 minutes.

5. Serve the tenders warm with the ranch dressing for dipping.

butttermilk ranch

MAKES ABOUT ½ CUP

⅓ cup **full-fat buttermilk** or kefir

3 tablespoons **sour cream**

2 tablespoons **mayonnaise**

1 teaspoon finely chopped **fresh dill**

1 teaspoon finely chopped **fresh parsley**

1 teaspoon finely chopped **fresh chives**

1 **garlic clove**, minced

½ teaspoon Dijon mustard

½ teaspoon **kosher salt**

½ tablespoon Crystal Hot Sauce

In a small bowl, whisk together the buttermilk, sour cream, mayonnaise, dill, parsley, chives, garlic, mustard, salt, and hot sauce, until smooth. Store in a an airtight container in the refrigerator for up to a week.

beef, with a little pork & lamb

If chicken is our go-to everyday meat, then the recipes in this chapter are for those slightly more special occasions. We say "slightly" because, honestly, we can easily find any reason special enough to celebrate with one of these dishes. The red-meat scale definitely tips toward the beef cuts (because that is what we love most), but we are excited to share with you some of our favorite ways to prepare pork and lamb, as well.

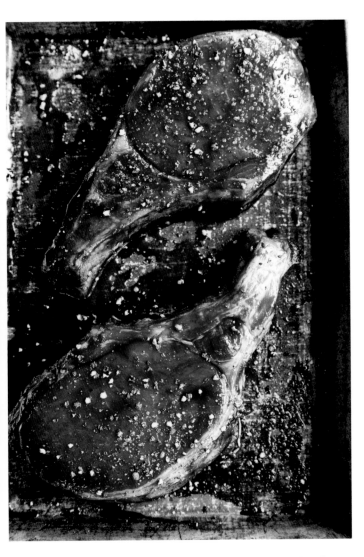

**molasses & coffee pork chops
with wilted radicchio**

coconut–ginger braised short ribs

Short ribs are so decadent and rich by their very nature they benefit from a punchy sauce. (By the way, I have renamed vodka martinis "Punchy Sauce." Give me one and you'll see why.) Taking the time to sear all sides of the short ribs is so important here. If you are working in batches, that requires about fifteen minutes of standing in front of the stove; but trust me—you will be rewarded when you deglaze the pan after those bad boys are done. The punchy sauce of citrus, ginger, and coconut comes together on its own in the two and a half hours the ribs are in the oven, during which time you get to help yourself to your own punchy sauce. ~ Julie

note

"English-cut" short ribs are ribs that have been cut along the bone, with meat on either side, and then cut across the bone to make 2- or 3-inch blocks (or just about) of meat. The other main style of cut is called "flanken" or "kalbi," in which the ribs are cut across the bone and usually thinly sliced, as done for Korean barbecue. And that concludes today's meat lecture.

- 3½ to 4 pounds bone-in **English-cut beef short ribs**, in 2- to 3-inch pieces (see Note)
- 1 tablespoon **kosher salt**, plus more as needed
- 1 teaspoon **freshly ground black pepper**, plus more as needed
- 3 tablespoons **grapeseed** or **canola oil**
- 1 large **onion**, quartered
- 4 large **carrots**, cut on an angle into 2-inch slices
- 2 tablespoons minced **fresh ginger**
- 6 **garlic cloves**, chopped
- 1 **jalapeño** or **Thai chile**, finely chopped, plus more for garnish
- 1 teaspoon **anise seeds**, or 2 **star anise**
- 1 tablespoon **paprika**
- 2 tablespoons **tomato paste**
- ½ cup **fresh orange juice**
- ½ cup plus 1 to 2 tablespoons **rice wine vinegar** or **apple cider vinegar**
- 3 tablespoons **fish sauce**
- 3 cups **beef** or **chicken broth**
- 1 (14-ounce) can **unsweetened full-fat coconut milk**
- 1 tablespoon **sorghum syrup, brown sugar,** or **honey**
- Sliced **scallion**, white and green parts
- Chopped **fresh cilantro**
- Cooked **rice, polenta,** or **mashed potatoes**, warmed

1. Season the short ribs all over with the 1 tablespoon salt and 1 teaspoon pepper. Let the ribs come to room temperature before searing, about 1 hour.

2. Preheat the oven to 325°F.

3. Pat the ribs dry with paper towels. In a Dutch oven or large, heavy-bottomed ovenproof pot, heat the oil over medium-high heat until shimmering. Working in batches, brown the short ribs on all sides, turning occasionally, until a dark golden crust forms all over, 15 to 20 minutes total. Transfer the ribs to a rimmed baking sheet or plate. Pour off all but 1 tablespoon of the rendered fat.

4. Add the onion and carrots to the pot, season with a generous pinch of salt and pepper, and cook until the onion is just starting to soften and turn golden brown, about 4 minutes. Add the ginger, garlic, jalapeño, anise seeds, and paprika and sauté until fragrant, 1 to 2 minutes. Stir in the tomato paste until it begins to caramelize on the bottom of the pot and the vegetables are well coated, about 2 minutes. Add the orange juice, ½ cup vinegar, the fish sauce, broth, coconut milk, and sorghum syrup. Stir to scrape up any browned bits from the bottom of the pot. Bring the liquid to a boil, then remove the pot from the heat.

5. Nestle the seared ribs, bone side up, in the braising liquid, making sure they are completely submerged. Tightly cover the pot with a sheet of foil, then place the lid on top. Transfer the pot to the oven and cook for 2 to 2½ hours, or until the meat is very tender and a fork inserted into the beef meets little to no resistance.

6. Transfer the ribs and carrots to a rimmed baking sheet or plate. Strain the braising liquid and discard the solids. Pour the sauce back into the pot and bring to a simmer over medium-high heat. Cook until reduced by one-third, about 12 minutes. Stir in 1 to 2 more tablespoons of vinegar and season to taste with more salt and pepper. Return the ribs and carrots to the sauce, turn off the heat, and cover the pot. Let the ribs sit in the sauce for 30 minutes.

7. Uncover and skim off any excess fat that has risen to the surface, then ladle the ribs, carrots, and sauce into shallow bowls and garnish with the scallions, cilantro, and more jalapeño, if desired. Serve with rice, polenta, or mashed potatoes.

lamb meatballs

I'm such a neat freak in the kitchen that I once covered the area around my stove with paper towels while frying meatballs, so as to avoid splatter. Turns out, grease-covered paper towels are highly flammable, so this was a very bad idea. (Thank you, Los Angeles Fire Department.) Luckily, there's a better way to avoid a greasy stove when making meatballs: bake 'em!

Now, we don't pretend to be experts on the flavors of Greek cuisine, but these meatballs and spiced yogurt definitely borrow from that region. As to what to eat with these, the spiced yogurt gives them tangy creaminess. And the light and fresh herb salad is a tribute to my friend Reed (@revival_roots on Instagram), who is in the business of creating vegetable gardens for people. Together we turned an awkward section of my backyard into a horticultural oasis. Okay, I didn't really help, but I did pick out what to grow. After working out of town one summer, I came home to find the garden bursting with lush growth, so I created this nearly all-herb salad. ~Jesse

MEATBALLS

Grapeseed oil or **nonstick cooking spray**

1½ pounds **ground lamb**

1 tablespoon finely chopped **fresh thyme**

1 tablespoon chopped **fresh parsley**

2 **garlic cloves**, minced

Finely gated zest of 1 **lemon**

3 ounces (½ cup) crumbled **feta cheese**

1 teaspoon **ground cumin**

1½ teaspoons **kosher salt**

½ teaspoon **freshly ground black pepper**

1 cup **panko bread crumbs**

SPICED YOGURT

1 cup plain **full-fat Greek yogurt**

2 tablespoons minced **red onion**

2 teaspoons finely chopped **fresh mint**

2 teaspoons finely chopped **fresh parsley**

1½ teaspoons **dried sumac**, or finely grated zest of ½ **lemon**

1¼ teaspoons **kosher salt**

Juice of ½ **lemon**

Herb Salad (recipe follows)

1. Make the meatballs: Preheat the oven to 425°F. Line a baking sheet with foil and coat with a bit of oil.

2. In a large bowl, combine the ground lamb, thyme, parsley, garlic, lemon zest, feta, cumin, salt, pepper, and bread crumbs. Mix with your hands until everything is just blended. Roll the lamb mixture into 1½-inch balls; don't overpack, or the meatballs will be tough. Place the meatballs on the baking sheet, spacing evenly. Bake until cooked through and starting to brown, about 20 minutes.

3. Make the spiced yogurt: In a medium bowl, stir together the yogurt, red onion, mint, parsley, sumac, salt, and lemon juice until well combined.

4. Serve the meatballs with the spiced yogurt and herb salad.

recipe continues . . .

herb salad

SERVES 4 TO 6

DRESSING

1 tablespoon **apple cider vinegar**

1 teaspoon **honey**

1 teaspoon **Dijon mustard**

1 **garlic clove**, minced

3 tablespoons **olive oil**

Kosher salt and **freshly ground black pepper**

SALAD

1 cup **fresh parsley leaves**

½ cup **fresh cilantro leaves**

½ cup **fresh mint leaves**, torn

¼ cup roughly chopped **fresh dill**

2 tablespoons chopped **fresh chives**

½ **English cucumber** or 1 **Persian cucumber**, diced

1 cup **cooked quinoa**

¼ cup **pomegranate seeds**

Edible flowers (optional)

1. **Make the dressing:** In a medium bowl, whisk together the vinegar, honey, mustard, and garlic. Slowly whisk in the olive oil until the dressing is emulsified. Season with salt and pepper.

2. **Make the salad:** Add the parsley, cilantro, mint, dill, chives, cucumber, quinoa, and pomegranate seeds to the salad bowl. Toss well to coat. Gently place the flowers on top, if using.

molasses & coffee pork chops

I love country ham! That sweet and smoky combination really reminds me of family reunions and gatherings back home. My grandpa Gordon Homer Nicolas had a smokehouse on his property so he smoked his own meat, but there are simpler ways to achieve that depth of flavor that don't involve building a structure in your backyard. You can use liquid smoke (which I stopped buying after my kids knocked a bottle off the pantry shelf, making my kitchen smell like an ashtray for an entire spring). Or, you can achieve it the way we do here: with a blend of spices (cumin, paprika, and ginger), molasses, and yes, brewed coffee. ~ Julie

½ cup **hot brewed coffee**

¼ cup **molasses** (preferably not blackstrap)

1 tablespoon **kosher salt**

1 tablespoon **brown sugar**

2 **garlic cloves**, smashed

½ teaspoon **ground cumin**

½ teaspoon **paprika**

½ teaspoon **ground ginger**

1 **dried bay leaf**

2 tablespoons **olive oil**

2 (6- to 8-ounce) **bone-in pork chops**, about 1 inch thick

1 head of **radicchio** (about 1 pound), quartered, cored, and roughly chopped

1 tablespoon **balsamic vinegar**

1. In a medium bowl, whisk together the coffee, molasses, salt, brown sugar, garlic, cumin, paprika, ginger, bay leaf, and 1 tablespoon of the olive oil. Let the marinade sit at room temperature until lukewarm or cool, about 3 minutes.

2. Add the pork chops to a large zippered plastic bag, then pour the marinade over the chops, close the bag, and massage to coat. Marinate in the refrigerator for at least 2 hours and up to 24 hours.

3. Thirty minutes prior to cooking, remove the pork chops from the marinade and let sit at room temperature.

4. Pour the marinade into a medium saucepan. Bring to a boil over medium-high heat, then reduce the heat to medium low and simmer, stirring occasionally, until thick and syrupy and reduced in volume by about two-thirds, about 10 minutes. Remove the bay leaf and garlic and cover to keep the reduced marinade warm while you cook the pork chops.

5. Heat the remaining tablespoon of olive oil in a large cast-iron skillet over medium-high heat until hot and shimmering. Pat the pork chops dry with paper towels, then sear until a nice dark brown crust forms, 4 to 5 minutes on each side. Scatter the radicchio in the pan around and on top of the chops and cook until the radicchio just begins to wilt, another 3 minutes. Add the balsamic vinegar and stir to coat the radicchio. Continue cooking, stirring the radicchio occasionally and turning the chops as needed to prevent burning, until the internal temperature of the pork chops reaches 145°F and the radicchio is wilted, 2 to 3 minutes more.

6. Transfer the pork chops and radicchio to a platter and let rest for 5 minutes. Drizzle the reduced marinade on top and serve.

camping chili

Every December, my dad would drive me and my siblings three hours outside of the city to cut our annual Christmas tree. All you needed was a permit that you could purchase for ten dollars. I told my dad there were tons of perfectly shaped trees in the grocery store parking lot for twenty bucks more, but he was always one for a bargain and a road trip.

My mom would often stay behind and enjoy a day without kids (a.k.a. a bath and reading the latest Danielle Steel) while we spent hours hiking around the woods looking for a suitable tree. I usually spotted one within the first fifteen minutes, but my dad would always say, "Let's mark it and keep on looking." My brother and sister were always supportive of his desire to extend the search. Inevitably, we would lose track of the perfect tree we had spotted at 2 p.m., and as the sun was setting at 6 p.m. my dad would panic and start chopping down whatever we could see in the fading light—which is how we ended up with Christmas bushes several years in a row.

As a kid, it felt like an eternity to be trapped in the wilderness. In my head, we barely survived on my mom's beef chili that she would pack for us in a thermos. Looking back upon those years, I realize that I was a dramatic "indoor kid," and my dad was great for making us all spend that time together. The chili my mom made will always remind me of him and the Christmas tree outings—and that I'm still an indoor person. But I do love a lumberjack plaid shirt and a fancy thermos.

Oh, and canned beans are fine here; that's what my mom always used. In the spirit of Anne Ferguson, use canned! ~ Jesse

- 3 tablespoons **grapeseed** or **canola oil**
- 2 pounds 85/15 **ground beef**
- 1 large **white onion**, diced
- 5 **garlic cloves**, minced
- 1 **jalapeño**, minced
- 2 teaspoons **dried Mexican oregano** (see Note, page 140)
- 1½ teaspoons **ground cumin**
- ½ teaspoon **smoked paprika**
- ½ teaspoon **ground coriander**
- ¼ teaspoon **ancho chile powder**
- 2 canned **chipotles in adobo**, chopped, plus 1 tablespoon **adobo sauce**
- ¼ cup **tomato paste**
- 2 tablespoons **Worcestershire sauce**
- 1 tablespoon **kosher salt**, plus more as needed
- ½ teaspoon **ground white pepper**, plus more as needed
- 1 (12-ounce) bottle **Modelo Negra** or other lager-style beer
- 1 (15-ounce) can **red kidney beans**, drained and rinsed
- 1 (15-ounce) can **black** or **pinto beans**, drained and rinsed
- 1 (28-ounce) can **crushed tomatoes**
- 4 cups **beef broth**
- Sliced **scallions**, green and white parts
- Shredded **cheese**
- Sour cream

1. Heat 2 tablespoons of the oil in a Dutch oven or large, heavy-bottomed pot over medium heat until shimmering. Add the ground beef and cook, breaking up with a wooden spoon, until no longer pink, 8 to 10 minutes. Transfer the beef to a colander to drain.

2. Heat the remaining tablespoon oil in the pot, then add the onion, garlic, and jalapeño and cook until the onion is translucent, about 5 minutes. Add the oregano, cumin, paprika, coriander, chile powder, chipotles, adobo sauce, tomato paste, Worcestershire sauce, 1 tablespoon salt, and ½ teaspoon white pepper. Stir to coat the vegetables and cook until fragrant, about 1 minute. Pour in the beer and bring to a simmer, then cook for 2 minutes. Add the beef to the pot along with the beans, tomatoes, and broth. Bring to a boil, then reduce the heat to medium low and gently simmer, uncovered, until thickened, about 1 hour, stirring occasionally. Season to taste with more salt and white pepper.

3. Ladle the chili into bowls (or a thermos). When ready to serve, top with scallions, shredded cheese, and sour cream.

chile relleno meatloaf

I love you, meatloaf, but I hate your name. Meat*loaf?* Really? Has there ever been a less appealing name for a dish? Let's think of some alternatives: meatbun? meatmass? Yeah, I guess "meatloaf" is the best option. The thing is, a well-made meatlump (nope!) is delicious. My mom made a low-rent but nonetheless delectable version covered in ketchup and Frito-Lay Funyuns. It wasn't going to win a beauty pageant, but who cares? It was going to be devoured before the rest of the contestants arrived, anyhow.

Julie and I racked our brains considering how to bring our version of the meatslab (absolutely not!) to this book. We think we cracked the "loaf" problem with this interpretation of the classic recipe. We borrow the flavors from a traditional beef- and cheese-filled chile relleno. And we think this union makes for a delicious meat . . . loaf. ~Jesse

MEATLOAF

Nonstick cooking spray

2 tablespoons **olive oil**

1 medium **onion**, diced

3 **garlic cloves**, minced

1 tablespoon **ancho chile powder**

1½ teaspoons **ground cumin**

1 teaspoon **dried Mexican oregano** (see Note, page 140)

1 tablespoon **Worcestershire sauce**

½ cup **plain bread crumbs**

½ cup **whole milk**

2 pounds **ground beef, pork,** or **veal,** or a combination

1 large or 2 small roasted **poblano chiles,** chopped (see Note)

1½ cups shredded **Monterey jack** or **Oaxacan cheese** (about 5 ounces)

¼ cup chopped **fresh cilantro**

1 large **egg,** lightly beaten

1 tablespoon **kosher salt**

2 teaspoons **freshly ground black pepper**

GLAZE

¼ cup jarred **tomato sauce**

¼ cup **ketchup**

2 tablespoons **honey**

1 tablespoon **Worcestershire sauce**

1. **Make the meatloaf:** Preheat the oven to 350°F. Lightly coat a 9 by 5-inch loaf pan with nonstick cooking spray.

2. Heat the olive oil in a small saucepan over medium-low heat. When the oil is hot, add the onion and cook until just soft, 3 to 4 minutes. Add the garlic and continue to cook until fragrant, about 1 minute. Add the chile powder, cumin, and oregano and continue cooking, stirring to make sure

the chile powder doesn't burn, until the mixture is very soft and slightly darkened, about 2 minutes more. Deglaze the pan with the Worcestershire sauce, scraping up all the bits from the bottom of the pan. Transfer to a large bowl and let cool slightly.

3. In a small bowl, combine the bread crumbs and milk and let soak for 5 minutes, until the milk is absorbed.

4. To the bowl with the onion mixture, add the ground meat, the soaked bread crumbs, roasted poblano, cheese, cilantro, egg, salt, and pepper. Mix thoroughly by hand until the mixture sticks to your fingers. Transfer the meat to the baking pan. Smooth the top and gently tap the loaf pan on the counter to make sure everything is snug.

5. Bake the meatloaf, uncovered, until brown on top and bubbly around the edges, 35 to 40 minutes.

6. Make the glaze: In a medium bowl, mix the tomato sauce, ketchup, honey, and Worcestershire sauce until smooth.

7. Remove the meatloaf from the oven and brush the glaze evenly on the top. Return to the oven and bake the meatloaf until an instant-read thermometer inserted in the center reads 155°F, another 30 to 35 minutes.

8. Set the meatloaf in the pan on a wire rack. Let cool for 15 minutes before slicing. As the meatloaf cools, pan juices will accumulate at the edges of the loaf in the pan. You have two options: pour out some of the accumulated juices and discard, or save the juices and drizzle on the meatloaf slices or on mashed potatoes served alongside.

note

If you can't find store-bought roasted poblanos, they are easy to replicate at home. Method 1: Place the chiles on a baking sheet and broil 4 to 6 inches from the heat for about 10 minutes, keeping an eye on them and occasionally turning them with tongs until blackened all over. Method 2: Using a gas range, char each chile directly over a burner set on high flame, turning with tongs as it blackens. After you have roasted the chiles, wrap them in foil while still hot and place in a plastic bag. Let the chiles rest for about 10 minutes (this will help loosen the skins), then use your fingers to peel off the skins. Discard the seeds and stem along with the skins.

crispy pork loin

SERVES
4

WITH GREEN
CHILE CHUTNEY

My birthday always comes during the Albuquerque International Balloon Festival, an incredible nine-day event when hundreds of hot-air balloons take to the skies in a breathtaking display of grandeur. A few years ago, Justin and I hosted a group of friends in Albuquerque to celebrate my birthday and enjoy this eighth wonder of the world. We stayed at one of my favorite places on the planet, Los Poblanos Historic Inn and Organic Farm. It's not only charming AF, but it also has some of the best food we've ever found in New Mexico. One of the things Julie and I discovered while we were there was a tangy and spicy Hatch green chile jam. We ate it like monsters, devouring a whole jar of it with bread and cheese while frantically listing all the other things we could put the jam on top of. "Crispy breaded pork loin medallions!" made us scream the loudest, so we created our own version of this peppery, chutney-like jam. It comes together surprisingly quickly, making this preparation a favorite weeknight dinner staple. ~Jesse

GREEN CHILE CHUTNEY

2 tablespoons **grapeseed** or **canola oil**
1 medium **shallot**, chopped
1 **garlic clove**, minced
1 teaspoon chopped **jalapeño**, seeded if desired
2 tablespoons **sugar**
1 tablespoon **apple cider vinegar**
1 (4-ounce) can diced **Hatch green chiles**
½ teaspoon **kosher salt**
½ teaspoon **ground cumin**

PORK MEDALLIONS

¼ cup **all-purpose flour**
1 teaspoon **ground cumin**
1 teaspoon **paprika**
1 teaspoon **kosher salt**
½ teaspoon **freshly ground black pepper**
2 large **eggs**
1¼ cups **panko bread crumbs**
6 boneless **pork medallions** (about 1 pound), pounded to ⅓-inch thickness
½ cup **canola** or **grapeseed oil**

1. Make the chutney: In a small saucepan, heat the oil over medium heat. When the oil is shimmering, add the shallot, garlic, and jalapeño and cook until softened, 2 to 3 minutes. Add the sugar and stir until dissolved, 1 minute. Add the vinegar and green chiles and cook, stirring, until thickened and jammy, 3 to 4 minutes. Stir in the salt and cumin, then remove the pan from the heat. (Makes about ½ cup.)

2. Make the pork: In a shallow bowl or pie pan, stir together the flour, cumin, paprika, salt, and pepper. Lightly beat the eggs in another shallow bowl. Add the panko to a third shallow bowl. Coat the pork medallions in the flour mixture, then in the egg, then in the panko.

3. Heat the oil in a large sauté pan or skillet over medium heat until it is shimmering. Working in batches to avoid overcrowding the pan, add the breaded pork and cook until golden brown on both sides, about 3 minutes per side. Transfer to a paper towel–lined plate to drain.

4. Serve the pork with the chutney spooned on top.

grilled skirt steak

SERVES
6 TO 8

WITH
PINEAPPLE
SALSA

Did we mention that the idea for this cookbook came from a blog we started called "Julie and Jesse Cook"? (I know, I know; the title is pretty amazing. Don't ask us how we came up with it. It was a stroke of genius that neither of us has been able to top.) Anyhow, this is adapted from one of the first recipes we created together for the blog. It's a flavorful, spicy, and citrusy carne asada–like grilled steak. We are more experienced now, so we have given the original concept a bit of an overhaul with this grilled pineapple salsa, but the spirit of the early creation is still alive and well here. ~J&J

1 large **pineapple**, peeled, cored, and sliced into 1-inch-thick rounds
1 small **jalapeño**, stemmed and seeded
2 canned **chipotle chiles in adobo**
Juice of 2 **limes**
¼ cup **olive oil**
2 tablespoons **soy sauce**
2 tablespoons **fish sauce**
6 **garlic cloves**
1 cup **fresh cilantro**, leaves and tender stems

1½ teaspoons **ground cumin**
½ teaspoon **ground coriander**
2 tablespoons **brown sugar**
½ teaspoon **kosher salt**
¼ teaspoon **ground white pepper**
2 pounds **skirt steak** (2 to 3 whole steaks), trimmed and cut with the grain into 5- to 6-inch-wide pieces
Grapeseed or **canola oil**, for greasing
Flour tortillas, warmed (optional)

1. In the bowl of a food processor or blender, combine one of the pineapple rounds, the jalapeño, chipotle chiles, lime juice, olive oil, soy sauce, fish sauce, garlic, cilantro, cumin, coriander, brown sugar, salt, and pepper. Blend until mostly smooth, about 1 minute. Transfer ¼ cup of the marinade to a small bowl, cover, and refrigerate (this will get tossed with the pineapple salsa).

2. Pour the remaining marinade into a large zippered plastic bag or container with a lid and place the steaks in the marinade. Massage to coat completely, then refrigerate for at least 3 hours, or up to overnight.

3. Remove the steaks from the refrigerator 30 to 40 minutes prior to cooking and allow them to come to room temperature. Preheat a grill or grill pan to high heat for 10 minutes. Grease the grates lightly with a folded-up paper towel dipped in oil, using tongs to hold the paper towel.

4. Grill the remaining pineapple rounds until they are marked with deep golden grill marks, about 4 minutes per side. Transfer the grilled pineapple to a cutting board and cut into 1-inch pieces, then transfer to a medium bowl. Pour the reserved marinade over the pineapple and stir to coat.

5. Remove the steaks from the marinade and gently shake off any excess liquid. Place the steaks on the hot grill. If using a gas grill, cover; if using a grill pan or charcoal grill, leave exposed. Cook until well charred on one side, 2 to 3 minutes, then flip and continue to cook until the steaks reach your desired doneness, another 3 to 4 minutes (see page 15). Transfer the steaks to a cutting board, tent with foil, and let rest for 10 minutes.

6. Thinly slice the steak pieces against the grain. Serve the steak with the pineapple salsa and with warm flour tortillas, if desired.

fennel–rubbed spare ribs

There are so many different kinds of ribs, and I've always associated all of them with saucy and sticky BBQ that leaves you looking like a toddler eating pasta for the first time. To be honest, as a person who doesn't love getting messy when I eat, I was never into making ribs at home—that was until my mom taught me how to slow-roast the ribs wrapped in aluminum foil. Seasoned with just a fennel dry rub—no sauce—these spare ribs stay super tender and … ugh, I said I wouldn't use this word in the book: moist! This meal is proof that you can be a bit fancy without a ton of work. And also without a bib. ~ Julie

1 (2½- to 3-pound) rack of **pork spare ribs**, membrane removed (see Note)

2 teaspoons **kosher salt**

1 teaspoon **freshly ground black pepper**

2 tablespoons **fennel seeds**, coarsely crushed

2 tablespoons '**Que Dust** (page 69), plus more for serving

4 sprigs of **fresh thyme**

l. Preheat the oven to 325°F.

2. Pat the ribs dry with paper towels and season with the salt and pepper.

3. In a small bowl, mix the fennel seeds and 'Que Dust. Rub the spice mix all over the ribs so they are well coated, including the sides and ends. Place the thyme sprigs on a long sheet of aluminum foil and place the ribs, meaty side up, on top of the thyme. Wrap the foil tightly around the ribs. Wrap the ribs again tightly in another long sheet of foil. Place on a rimmed baking sheet and bake until the meat is tender, 2 hours. Remove the ribs from the oven and let rest, still wrapped, for 10 minutes.

4. Switch the oven to broil, unwrap the ribs, and broil close to the heat until nicely browned and crisp in spots.

5. Slice the rack into individual ribs, place on a serving platter, and drizzle any accumulated juices on top. Sprinkle with more 'Que Dust, if desired.

note

You'll want to remove the membrane from the underside of the ribs because it won't get tender after cooking. This is super easy and takes only a few seconds. Use a sharp paring knife to cut down the middle of each rib bone. Loosen the membrane at one end, and then use a paper towel to grab the membrane and pull it off.

ribeye steak

When I was growing up, steakhouses were places my family went on special occasions. First Communion? Steakhouse afterward. Mother's Day? Let's go to the steakhouse! My final, triumphant performance as Lost Boy #5 in *Peter Pan* at the Albuquerque Civic Light Opera? Celebrate that career high at the steakhouse. I should clarify that when I say "steakhouse," I'm talking about Sizzler. Nowadays, I love grabbing a steak at a fancier establishment, but when I don't feel like putting pants on, I bring the steakhouse home and cook a ribeye steak. Because of all the fat on them, ribeye steaks are difficult to ruin, and the chipotle lime butter offers that punch of Southwestern spice! ~**Jesse**

1 bone-in **ribeye steak**, 1¼ to 1½ inches thick (about 1 pound)

2 teaspoons **kosher salt**

1 teaspoon **freshly ground black pepper**

2 tablespoons **grapeseed** or **canola oil**

2 to 3 tablespoons **Chipotle Lime Butter** (page 263)

1. Set a wire rack inside a rimmed baking sheet or sheet pan. Place the steak on the rack and sprinkle the salt and pepper all over, including the edges. Allow the steak to sit at room temperature for 45 minutes.

2. Pat the steak dry with paper towels. Heat the oil in a large cast-iron skillet over high heat until just beginning to smoke. Add the steak and sear until a deep golden brown crust starts to develop, about 2 minutes. Flip the steak and sear on the other side until deep golden brown, another 2 minutes. Reduce the heat to medium and add 1 tablespoon of the chipotle lime butter to the pan. Gently swirl the pan to move the butter around and continue cooking the steak, flipping it a few times to cover the steak completely in butter, until the steak registers 125 to 130°F for medium-rare, or is done to your liking (see page 15), remembering that the temperature will rise a few degrees as the steak rests off heat.

3. Transfer the steak to a cutting board or plate, top with 1 to 2 more tablespoons of the chipotle lime butter and let rest for 10 minutes before slicing and serving.

beef tenderloin

Who doesn't love a one-pan dish? Three-pan Sally, that's who. We can't get over how easy this tenderloin is to make. The depth of flavor that it packs has no business being associated with such a low-maintenance meal! Delicious enough to be served at a holiday event and easy enough for a last-minute dinner, this feast is more reliable than a Japanese hybrid car.

The carrots participate in the spicy fun by borrowing a few spoonfuls of the peppy steak seasoning, but feel free to invite any of your favorite hearty veggies or roots to the party. Onions! Brussels sprouts! Parsnips! Mix and match—this dish can take it! ~ **J&J**

STEAK SEASONING

- 2 tablespoons **kosher salt**
- 1 tablespoon coarsely ground **black pepper**
- 1 tablespoon **garlic powder**
- 1 tablespoon **onion powder**
- 1 tablespoon **dried dill**
- 2 tablespoons **paprika**
- 1 tablespoon **ground coriander**
- ½ tablespoon **red pepper flakes**

BEEF TENDERLOIN AND CARROT FRIES

- 1½ teaspoons **kosher salt**
- 1 (2-pound) boneless **beef tenderloin**, trimmed and tied
- 2 tablespoons **olive oil**
- 1 pound **carrots**, cut into strips about 4 inches long and 1 inch wide
- 5 tablespoons **unsalted butter**
- 1 tablespoon **Worcestershire sauce**

1. Make the steak seasoning: In a small bowl or jar, mix the salt, pepper, garlic powder, onion powder, dill, paprika, coriander, and red pepper flakes. (Makes ½ cup. The seasoning will keep in an airtight container at room temperature for up to 1 year.)

2. Make the beef and carrots: Rub 1 tablespoon of the steak seasoning and 1 teaspoon of the salt evenly over the surface of the tenderloin. Let the meat sit at room temperature for about 30 minutes.

3. Preheat the oven to 400°F.

4. Heat 1 tablespoon of the olive oil in a large cast-iron skillet over medium-high heat. When the oil is hot and shimmering, sear the beef on all sides until golden brown, about 1 minute per side. Transfer the pan to the oven and roast for 15 minutes.

5. In a large bowl, toss the carrots with the remaining tablespoon olive oil and 1 tablespoon of the steak seasoning. Remove the skillet with the tenderloin from the oven, scatter the carrots around the beef, then return to the oven and continue to roast

for 10 to 15 minutes more, until the internal temperature of the tenderloin reaches 125 to 130°F for medium-rare. Using tongs, transfer the beef tenderloin to a cutting board and let rest for 10 minutes.

6. Meanwhile, melt the butter in a small bowl or saucepan, then stir in the Worcestershire sauce and the remaining ½ teaspoon salt. Arrange the carrots on a serving platter. Slice the tenderloin into 2-inch medallions and place on top of the carrots. Drizzle the Worcestershire butter over the steaks and serve.

lamb chops

Fancy, and it pulls together quickly. That's a description of me, not Julie "Molasses" Tanous. It's also a description of these lamb chops. Because they don't take a ton of time, they are perfect for a dinner party that Julie would probably be late for. Like many people, I discovered rhubarb in strawberry rhubarb pie. I love how it transforms from tart to sweet when cooked down, so it's a beautiful companion for lamb. Unlike a rack of lamb or a full leg, these chops cook very, very quickly. It's almost like magic!

~Jesse

- 8 loin or rib **lamb chops** (about 1½ pounds)
- 1 teaspoon **kosher salt**, plus more as needed
- ½ teaspoon **freshly ground black pepper**
- ½ teaspoon **ground cumin**
- 2 tablespoons **all-purpose flour**
- 2 tablespoons **unsalted butter**
- 2 tablespoons **canola oil**
- ½ cup **apple cider vinegar**
- ¾ cup **light brown sugar**
- 1 tablespoon **pomegranate molasses** (see Note)
- 1 teaspoon minced **fresh ginger**
- 1 **cinnamon stick**
- ¼ cup thinly sliced **red onion**
- 12 ounces (3 large stalks) **rhubarb**, cut into 1-inch pieces
- ¼ cup **fresh mint leaves**, torn

1. Pat the lamb chops dry with paper towels and let stand at room temperature for about 20 minutes.

2. Season the chops on both sides with the 1 teaspoon salt, the pepper, and cumin, then sprinkle with the flour. Pat to coat, shaking off the excess. Melt the butter and oil together in a large skillet over medium-high heat. Working in batches, sear the lamb chops until golden brown on one side, about 4 minutes, then flip and cook on the other side, basting in the butter mixture, until golden brown and the internal temperature reaches 130°F for medium-rare, 2 minutes more. Transfer to a rimmed

serving platter and loosely tent with foil.

3. Wipe out the skillet. Add the vinegar, brown sugar, and a couple pinches of salt and bring to a simmer over medium heat, stirring to dissolve the sugar. Add the molasses, ginger, cinnamon stick, and onion and cook until the onion is just starting to soften, about 5 minutes. Add the rhubarb and cook until softened, about 4 minutes. Remove the cinnamon stick, then spoon the rhubarb mixture and sauce over the lamb. Garnish with the mint. Serve warm.

pomegranate molasses

The sweet tang of pomegranate molasses is the perfect finish for so many dishes. We always try to have a bottle on hand in our pantry. It brings complex sweetness to homemade vinaigrettes and is delicious stirred into tea or drizzled over hummus. This syrup, an honored and essential ingredient in Middle Eastern cooking, can be found in most grocery stores or online, but if you are in a pinch and can't find any, may we suggest combining equal parts honey and lemon juice to stand in for that syrupy-tart punch? It won't achieve that distinct depth of flavor, but it is better than just leaving it out!

sopaipillas
~by Jesse

If you haven't traveled through New Mexico, the sopaipilla may be completely foreign to you. And if it is, I am so excited to introduce you to this delicious pillow of fried bread. Sopaipillas are believed to have been born almost 200 years ago in Albuquerque's Hispanic community. The great pride that the community has for this delicious pastry is proven by the fact that almost every New Mexican restaurant in Albuquerque serves sopaipillas as complimentary table bread. They are meant to be enjoyed as a way to mop up the extra sauce on your plate and to cut the heat of the spices that New Mexican food packs.

I spent a good portion of my high school years working as a host at one of Albuquerque's most popular restaurants, Sadie's Cocina. (If you are passing through, definitely pop in and tell Betty Jo I sent you.) After seating a table of guests, I would often take a detour by the line cooks, snag a sopaipilla, and devour it before returning to the host stand. (Let's take a moment here to honor the memory of my seventeen-year-old metabolism. It was a force of nature, and a day does not go by that I don't miss it.) I loved a "sopa"—that's what I called them. To this day I get excited when I see *sopa* on menus and am immediately disappointed when I am reminded that *sopa* means "soup" in Spanish.

The beauty of the sopaipilla is that it is so easy to transform from a side of bread into the foundation for a full-on meal. Use your wildest imagination and stuff those naughty little bread pillows with anything! (That sounded dirtier than I intended.) Spicy beef, cheesy scrambled eggs, whipped cream and chocolate sauce—they all work with the great sopaipilla!

sopaipillas
stuffed
with pulled
chicken
in red chile
sauce

sopaipillas

I was always intimidated by the idea of making sopaipillas at home. Maybe that's because the restaurant I used to work at had an entire section of the kitchen devoted to churning out these delicious, airy treats. Once I put my big boy pants on and attempted a batch, though, I realized just how easy they are. Start here with this basic sopaipilla recipe and then turn the page for a few ideas about how to upgrade them!

2 cups **all-purpose flour**, plus more as needed

2 teaspoons **sugar**

1 teaspoon **baking powder**

1 teaspoon **kosher salt**

2 tablespoons **vegetable shortening**

¾ cup **whole milk**, lukewarm (between 98° and 105°F)

Grapeseed or **canola oil**

1. In a large bowl, whisk together the flour, sugar, baking powder, and salt. Rub the shortening into the flour mixture with your fingers or a pastry cutter until the mixture resembles coarse meal. Stir in the milk until combined. Turn the dough out onto a clean surface and knead briefly (10 to 12 turns) to form a cohesive ball. The dough will be soft and slightly lumpy on the surface. Wipe out the bowl, then lightly coat it with a little oil. Transfer the dough back to the bowl, turn to coat all sides, then cover with plastic wrap and let stand for 20 minutes.

2. Flour a work surface, then roll out the dough to a 10 by 15-inch rectangle about ⅛ inch thick. Use a sharp knife or pizza cutter to cut the dough into a grid with 4 spaces in one direction and 3 spaces in the other direction, for a total of 12 rectangles.

3. Fit a large, heavy-bottomed pot or Dutch oven with a deep-fry thermometer. Pour in enough oil to reach a depth of 1½ inches. Heat the oil over medium-high heat until the temperature reaches 350°F. Line a baking sheet with paper towels and set nearby.

4. Working in batches of 3 to 4 at a time, gently lower the sopaipillas into the hot oil and fry, flipping once, until golden and puffed, 50 to 60 seconds per side. Using a slotted spoon, carefully remove the sopaipillas from the oil and transfer to the paper towel–lined baking sheet, then fry the remaining dough pieces.

breakfast sopaipillas

Those working as hosts at Sadie's Cocina were offered breakfast every morning. The choices were limited: scrambled eggs, bacon, maybe hash browns, but there was always the option for green chiles. That was all I needed to spruce up my eggs. To this day, green chiles are what I reach for when I am making a quick breakfast. So, I can't think of a more perfect way to start a Sunday morning than having a sopaipilla stuffed with cheesy scrambled eggs, crumbled bacon, and a spoonful of Hatch Green Chile Sauce (page 64.) I am not going to tell you how to scramble eggs, but I will tell you how I like to do them, which makes for extra-soft, creamy eggs. Pretty much everything else in this recipe is to taste.

Large **eggs** (1 or 2 per sopaipilla)

Half-and-half

Kosher salt and **freshly ground black pepper**

Unsalted butter

Grated cheese of choice (I like cheddar)

Hatch Green Chile Sauce (page 64)

Sopaipillas (page 197)

A few strips of **cooked bacon**, crumbled (optional)

1. Whisk the eggs in a bowl with a splash of half-and-half and a sprinkling of salt and pepper. Slowly cook the eggs in a nonstick pan with a little butter over low heat, adding the cheese when the eggs are about 1 minute out from being finished, which to me means when they're thick and custardy.

2. Drizzle with a few tablespoons of the chile sauce. Tear off a corner of each sopaipilla. Stuff the cheesy scramble into sopaipillas and add a bit of crumbled bacon, if using.

sopaipillas stuffed with pulled chicken in red chile sauce

"There's always more than one way to do it" will always be my motto when it comes to sopaipillas. Because they are served at almost every New Mexican restaurant, halfway through my meals there I would end up just stuffing the rest of my entree (usually green chile chicken enchiladas) into the sopaipillas and finishing that way. It was like having a bonus side dish at the end of dinner. Spicy ground beef, pulled pork, or our pulled chicken are just three ideas that come to mind—because there's always more than one way to stuff a sopaipilla!

Sopaipillas (page 107)
Pulled Chicken with New Mexican Red Chile Sauce (page 154), warmed

Toppings of choice (such as **shredded lettuce, diced tomatoes, sour cream, shredded cheese**)

Tear off a corner of a sopaipilla and fill it with a few tablespoons of the pulled chicken and sauce. Add toppings of choice and serve.

sopaipillas with powdered sugar & honey (or sorghum)

By this point, I think you understand that sopaipillas can be incredibly cooperative. If you don't understand that, then you aren't being very cooperative. Go back to the beginning of this section and begin again.

Transforming sopaipillas into a dessert can be done with gusto. Top them with ice cream, bananas, and caramel sauce; or drizzle them with chocolate sauce; or fill them with whipped cream and strawberries. My choice is always to enjoy them the way they were originally intended: simply with some powdered sugar and a generous drizzle of honey—or in Julie's honor, with sorghum.

Sopaipillas (page 107)

Confectioners' sugar
Honey or **sorghum** (or fruit or chocolate sauce or caramel sauce)

While the sopaipillas are still warm, sprinkle them with powdered sugar and drizzle with honey or sorghum (or your choice of sweet thing). Serve them warm.

gone fishin'

Living in the landlocked state of New Mexico, Jesse rarely ordered fish on a menu. But for Julie, who grew up vacationing in the Florida Panhandle, seafood is deeply nostalgic. (Probably not as nostalgic as the ocean is to the fish, if you ask them, but we digress.) And after living on the West Coast for fifteen years, Jesse has grown to have great affinity for delicious fish recipes. We promise we aren't fishing for compliments, but we are sure this collection of pescetarian delights will leave you hooked!

blackened fish sandwich

slow-roasted char

What's great about this dish is that you only have to do just enough: you bring together the creamy leeks on the stovetop, add the fish, pop it in the oven, and walk away. We also recommend going back for it eventually to eat it. Not only is this the perfect meal for a dinner party (low prep and tons of time to enjoy your company while the fish is roasting), but also it has become one of Justin's favorite ways to eat char or salmon. He is the king of "I'm trying [fill in the blank] this week." Here are some examples: "I'm trying 'not drinking wine' this week"; "I'm 'riding my bike twenty miles every day' this week"; "I'm trying 'telling people that I meditate' this week." On one of his "I'm not doing lactose this week" weeks I made him this for dinner, substituting clarified butter (page 262) in place of butter, and coconut cream in place of heavy cream. We still kept the white wine, because it wasn't one of his "I'm not doing wine this week" weeks. That being said, the original recipe is perfection. ~Jesse

- 2 tablespoons **unsalted butter**
- 3 medium **leeks**, white and light green parts only, cut in half lengthwise, then sliced into 1-inch-long half-moons and cleaned (see Note on page 134)
- 1 small **white onion**, chopped
- 2 **garlic cloves**, minced
- 1 teaspoon **dried thyme**
- 2 teaspoons **fennel seeds**, crushed
- **Kosher salt** and **freshly ground black pepper**
- 1/3 cup **dry white wine**
- 2/3 cup **heavy cream**
- 1/2 cup **vegetable broth**, plus more as needed
- Finely grated zest and juice of 1/2 **lemon**
- 4 (8-ounce) skinless fillets of **arctic char** or **salmon**

1. Preheat the oven to 300°F.

2. Melt the butter in a large ovenproof skillet over medium-high heat. Add the leeks, onion, garlic, thyme, and fennel seeds and stir to coat. Season with salt and pepper and cook, stirring occasionally, until the vegetables just begin to soften, about 2 minutes. Add the wine and cook, stirring occasionally, until most of the liquid has evaporated, 3 to 5 minutes. Add the cream, 1/2 cup broth, and lemon zest and juice and simmer, stirring occasionally, until the leeks are soft and the cream has thickened, about 15 minutes. Add a little more broth as needed if the leeks look dry. Season to taste with more salt and pepper.

3. Season the fish fillets on both sides with salt and pepper, then nestle them in the creamy leeks. Move the skillet to the oven and roast until the fish is opaque and flakes easily when nudged with a fork, about 25 minutes. Serve warm.

blackened fish sandwich

The powdered-sugar sands of the Emerald Coast on the Florida Panhandle was where my family loved to vacation, and a dive bar, the High Tide, was one of my parents' favorite places to eat. Maybe it was because it was the type of joint that didn't care if you bellied up to the bar with an eleven-year-old. When I would enter the dimly lit place, the scent of beer and sea water made me feel I had joined the world of grownups.

The menu was simple and showcased the local coastal flavors: the catch of the day with three choices—blackened, grilled, or fried. The adults inevitably would go for whatever they were serving blackened, so in an attempt to seem more mature, I would follow suit. Even to this day, the peppery heat of blackened fish takes me right back to my stool at the bar of the High Tide. ~ **Julie**

QUICK SLAW

¼ medium head of **green cabbage**, finely shredded

1 **celery stalk**, finely chopped

¼ cup **mayonnaise**

Juice of ½ **lemon**

Kosher salt and **freshly ground black pepper**

SANDWICHES

1¼ tablespoons **smoked paprika**

2 teaspoons **kosher salt**

1 teaspoon **freshly ground black pepper**

½ teaspoon **lemon pepper**

1 teaspoon **onion powder**

1 teaspoon **garlic powder**

½ teaspoon **dried thyme**

½ teaspoon **dried tarragon**

¼ teaspoon **cayenne pepper**

4 (4- to 6-ounce) **fish fillets** (such as amberjack, grouper, mackerel, mahi mahi, ocean trout, or striped bass)

4 tablespoons (½ stick) **unsalted butter**, melted

2 tablespoons **grapeseed** or **canola oil**

4 **rolls**, halved

Sliced **tomato, onion,** and **pickles**, for serving (optional)

1. **Make the slaw:** In a medium bowl, toss the cabbage and celery with the mayonnaise and lemon juice until well coated. Season to taste with salt and black pepper.

2. **Make the sandwiches:** In a small bowl, whisk together the paprika, salt, black pepper, lemon pepper, onion powder, garlic powder, thyme, tarragon, and cayenne.

3. Line a baking sheet with aluminum foil. Brush both sides of the fish fillets with the melted butter, then place on the baking sheet. Reserve the remaining melted butter. Sprinkle the seasoning on both sides of the fillets.

4. Heat the oil in a large stainless-steel or well-seasoned cast-iron pan over medium-high heat until hot and shimmering. Carefully transfer the fish to the hot pan and cook until darkened in color, 2 to 3 minutes. Use a fish spatula to gently flip the fish. Pour the reserved melted butter all over the fish and continue cooking until the second side is blackened and the fish is just opaque throughout, another 2 to 3 minutes.

5. Preheat the broiler on high. Arrange the buns cut-side up on a baking sheet. Place under the broiler and toast until deep golden brown.

6. Place a fish fillet on each bun, mound some coleslaw on top, drizzle with blackened butter from the pan, then add the bun tops, and serve warm with garnishes, if desired.

crispy-skin salmon

SERVES
4

WITH MARINATED ARTICHOKE HEARTS

Crispy-skin salmon: approachable, adaptable, easy to work with, and something almost everyone likes. It's the Tom Hanks of protein. I'll be honest with you; for years I was a die-hard advocate of removing the fish skin before cooking it because I was completely incapable of achieving the desired "potato chip" crispness I knew it needed. That was until Julie taught me the proper method. The secret is to not only sear the skin side in oil at high temperature but also to leave it undisturbed for a few minutes, letting the fish basically cook through before flipping it over. I pair this fish with countless companions. To tie up the Tom Hanks analogy, this salmon has great chemistry and is well liked by most everything that it comes in contact with. We've cast it with artichoke hearts here, but our list of dream partners also includes Tomato Confit Pasta (page 145), or Grilled Cabbage Coleslaw (page 194), to name just a few. ~Jesse

4 (6-ounce) skin-on **salmon** or **arctic char fillets**
Kosher salt and **freshly ground black pepper**
2 tablespoons **grapeseed** or **olive oil**
1 **garlic clove**, minced
1 medium **shallot**, minced
2 (12-ounce) jars marinated **artichoke hearts**

1 (6-ounce) can pitted **green manzanilla olives**, drained
Finely grated zest and juice of 1 **lemon**
½ cup **fish** or **vegetable broth**
1 cup **fresh spinach** or **sorrel**
Chopped **fresh parsley** or **cilantro**

1. Heat a large skillet over medium heat for about 3 minutes. While the pan heats, pat the salmon dry with paper towels and season the skin with salt and pepper.

2. Heat the oil in the skillet until hot and shimmering, then add the salmon, skin-side down, and gently press the fish with a fish spatula for about 10 seconds to make sure the skin makes even contact with the hot pan. Cook the salmon until the skin is golden brown and super crispy to the touch, 4 to 6 minutes. Transfer the salmon, skin side up, to a plate.

3. Add the garlic and shallot to the pan and sauté until translucent, 1 to 2 minutes. Add the artichokes and their liquid along with the olives. Cook until warmed through, about 3 minutes. Add the lemon zest and juice and the broth to the pan and bring to a simmer, about 1 minute, scraping up any browned bits from the bottom of the pan. Stir in the spinach, then nestle the salmon in the sauce, skin side up, and cook for 2 to 3 more minutes for medium/medium-rare, or until done to your liking. Remove the pan from the heat. Garnish with the parsley and serve.

crab linguine

I love crustaceans. But I hate the production that goes into eating them. There are certain people who love to work for their food; I'm not one of those people. If a meal requires me to cover my shirt with a bib, I'm already nervous. I'm accident prone as it is, and I don't need to add another element of danger. (There are thousands of lobster injuries every year in America; look it up!) If you are feeling confident, do your thing! Buy whole crabs and go for it. If you are like me, just get ready-to-go crab meat from your fishmonger. I hate myself for actually using the word "fishmonger," but it's just a person at the grocery store who sells fish. Don't ask me why they get their own title. It's especially confusing because in *Hamlet*, Shakespeare uses the word as a euphemism for a pimp. You know what show I miss? *Fishmonger My Ride.* ~**Jesse**

BREAD CRUMBS

1 cup torn **day-old baguette pieces**

2 tablespoons **olive oil**

¼ cup chopped **fresh tarragon** or **parsley**

½ teaspoon finely grated **lemon zest**

Kosher salt and **freshly ground black pepper**

CRAB LINGUINE

Kosher salt

8 ounces **linguine**

1 tablespoon **olive oil**, plus more as needed

1 tablespoon **unsalted butter**

1 medium **shallot**, finely chopped

3 **garlic cloves**, minced

¼ teaspoon **red pepper flakes**, plus more as needed

½ cup **cream cheese**, room temperature

Freshly ground black pepper

½ teaspoon finely grated **lemon zest**

Juice of 1 **lemon**

8 ounces jumbo **lump crab meat** (we love Dungeness), picked over for shell bits

1. **Make the bread crumbs:** Preheat the oven to 350°F. Line a baking sheet with aluminum foil.

2. Add the baguette pieces to a food processor and pulse until broken down into coarse crumbs, 5 to 10 seconds. Toss the bread crumbs with the olive oil and spread on the baking sheet in an even layer. Bake until golden brown and very crispy, about 20 minutes. Stir in the tarragon and lemon zest and season to taste with salt and pepper.

3. **Make the crab linguine:** Bring a large pot of salted water to a boil and cook the linguine until al dente, 7 to 9 minutes (or according to package directions). Reserve 1½ cups of the pasta water, then drain the pasta. Toss the pasta with a little olive oil to keep it from sticking together.

4. In a large skillet, melt the butter and the 1 tablespoon olive oil over medium heat. When it is hot and bubbly, add the shallot, garlic, and red pepper flakes and cook, stirring often, until soft and golden, 2 to 3 minutes. Add the cream cheese and cook until melty and the mixture is smooth, 2 to 3 minutes. Season to taste with a pinch of salt and pepper. Stir in the lemon zest and juice, crab meat, and about ¾ cup of the reserved pasta water. Cook until the sauce is thick and glossy and the crab is warmed through, 3 to 4 minutes, adding more pasta water as needed if the sauce is getting too thick. Stir in the linguine and half the bread crumbs and toss to combine. Transfer to a serving dish (or leave in the pan) and sprinkle the remaining bread crumbs on top.

gulf coast grouper & grits

Shrimp and grits is about as classically Southern a dish as you can get, and if you travel to coastal South Carolina, I encourage you to try it! But it's also my personal mission to show you that shrimp is not the be-all and end-all when it comes to grits. Gulf Coast grouper, a member of the sea bass family, is one of my favorites, but some other great options are black sea bass, flounder, branzino, or tilapia. For this dish, we spice the fish fillets with EveryBay Seasoning, our homemade version of Old Bay seasoning, sear them until golden, and serve them with classic grits. To finish, a spoonful (or three) of creamy spinach sauce adds a touch of Southern decadence. And by all means, if you wanna make this with shrimp, go for it.

~Julie

GRITS

4 cups **water**

1 teaspoon **kosher salt**

1 cup **stone-ground white grits** (not quick-cooking)

2 tablespoons **butter**

FLORENTINE SAUCE

1 tablespoon **olive oil**

1 **shallot**, finely chopped

2 **garlic cloves**, minced

1 sprig of **fresh thyme**

½ cup **dry white wine**

1½ cups **heavy cream**

1 teaspoon **EveryBay Seasoning** (page 262) or **Old Bay Seasoning**

1 teaspoon **kosher salt**

1 (10-ounce) bag **fresh spinach**, chopped

GROUPER

1 teaspoon **kosher salt**

1 teaspoon **black pepper**

1 tablespoon **EveryBay Seasoning** (page 262) or Old Bay Seasoning

2 pounds **grouper** or **halibut fillet** (1 inch thick), cut into 6 pieces

2 tablespoons **olive oil**, plus more as needed

1 **lemon**, sliced

1. Make the grits: In a medium saucepan, bring the water and salt to a boil. Whisk in the grits, then return to a boil. Reduce the heat to low, cover, and cook until the grits are tender, 20 to 30 minutes. If your grits are too thick or sticking to the pan, add a little water to make them creamy. Remove from the heat and stir in the butter. Cover to keep warm.

2. Make the sauce: In a medium saucepan, heat the olive oil over medium heat. When the oil is shimmering, add the shallot and garlic and sauté until softened, 2 to 3 minutes. Add the thyme and wine and bring to a simmer. Cook until the wine is reduced by half, 2 to 3 minutes. Add the cream, seasoning, and salt. Bring to a boil, then reduce the heat to medium low and simmer until the cream is reduced by one-third, 2 to 3 minutes. Add the spinach and cook until wilted, 2 minutes. Remove the pot from the heat and cover to keep warm. (Discard the thyme sprig.)

3. Make the grouper: In a small bowl, mix the salt, pepper, and seasoning. Lightly coat the fish with oil, then rub all over with the seasoning mixture.

1. In a large skillet, heat the 2 tablespoons olive oil over medium-high heat. When the oil is shimmering, add the fish. Gently press the fillets down with a spatula so they don't buckle. Cook until golden brown, about 4 minutes. Flip and cook on the other side until golden brown and cooked through, about 4 minutes.

5. Serve the fish and grits with the spinach and sauce on top and lemon slices alongside.

salmon patties

Jesse suggested renaming these "Salmon Croquettes," but I told him I could already hear my family calling me and saying, "Julie, what in the hell is a croquette? Just because you live in fancy Los Angeles and are cooking with that redheaded guy we saw on Ellen DeGeneres, that doesn't mean you have to go callin' a patty a croquette." And you know what? They're right. Stop trying to fancy me up, Jesse! This is exactly how my mom used to make these, so we are going to stick to the original name.

These *patties* are created with flaky canned salmon tossed with lemon juice and chopped fresh parsley, while the addition of cornmeal adds a perfect crunchy texture. Because they're so delicate and moist, it's best to let them sit in the fridge for half an hour before frying them, to keep the croquettes—sorry, patties—from breaking apart in the pan. No matter what you call them, we are certain you will fall in love with these bright little cakes! And okay, we do fancy them up a little bit with Meyer lemon tartar sauce, but regular old tartar sauce is fine! ~ **Julie**

1 (14.75-ounce) can **pink salmon**, drained and picked over for bones and skin

½ cup medium-grind **cornmeal**

2 tablespoons finely chopped **fresh parsley**

¼ cup **mayonnaise**

3 tablespoons grated **onion**

2 tablespoons **lemon juice**

Finely grated zest of 1 small **lemon**

1 large **egg**, lightly beaten

¾ teaspoon **kosher salt**, plus more as needed

¾ teaspoon **freshly ground pepper**

2 tablespoons **grapeseed** or **canola oil**

Meyer Lemon Tartar Sauce, for serving (page 157)

1. In a medium bowl, combine the salmon, cornmeal, parsley, mayonnaise, onion, lemon juice and zest, egg, ¾ teaspoon salt, and the pepper. Mix well with a fork, breaking up the salmon, until well combined. Scoop up a heaping ¼ cup of the salmon mixture and use your hands to gently shape into a rounded patty (like you're making crab cakes or burgers). Repeat with the rest of the salmon mixture. Place the patties on a plate, cover with plastic wrap, and refrigerate for 30 minutes.

2. In a large skillet, heat the oil over medium heat until shimmering. Place the patties in the hot oil and use a spatula to gently flatten them to about ¾-inch thickness. Cook until golden brown, 3 to 4 minutes, then gently flip over and cook until golden brown on the other side, another 3 minutes. Transfer to a paper towel–lined plate and sprinkle with a little additional salt and serve with the tartar sauce.

grilled swordfish

Fish and marinade can be tricky. You can't let the fish sit in lemon juice too long or the acidity will pickle the fish into a mushy texture. You can't let it hang out in sugar for an extended amount of time or it will burn in the cooking process. For something that literally lived its whole life in a giant marinade called the ocean, fish sure can be particular. That's why we love a reverse marinade. (Relax, we know it sounds like a gymnastics move—it's not.) This method of simply cooking the fish with just some olive oil, salt, and pepper, and then letting it hang out in a delicious marinade afterward allows the flavors to shine while not messing with the integrity of the swordfish. In this case, that marinade is a salty, tangy, umami-bomb potlikker—a.k.a. the liquid from braised greens. Round off, back handspring into a reverse marinade, and you'll stick the landing, taking home the Gold for the first time since 1988! ~ J&J

Grapeseed or **canola oil**, for greasing

4 (8-ounce) **swordfish steaks**, about 1 inch thick

Kosher salt and **freshly ground black pepper**

1 cup reserved **potlikker** from Braised Turnip Greens (page 179) or **vegetable broth**

3 **garlic cloves**, minced

1 tablespoon finely chopped **shallot**

Juice of 1 **lemon**

2 tablespoons **capers**, drained

1 tablespoon finely chopped **fresh oregano**

2 **anchovy fillets**, finely chopped

¼ cup sliced **Kalamata olives**

2 tablespoons **olive oil**

1. Preheat a grill or grill pan to medium-high heat and, using tongs, coat the grates with a paper towel dipped in a little oil.

2. Pat the swordfish dry and season on both sides with salt and pepper. Place on a plate and let sit at room temperature for about 15 minutes.

3. Add the potlikker, garlic, and chopped shallot to a small saucepan. Bring to a boil over high heat and cook, uncovered, until reduced by almost half, 7 to 8 minutes. Remove the pot from the heat and whisk in the lemon juice, capers, oregano, anchovies, and olives. Season with salt and pepper and let cool until it's very warm, but not too hot.

4. Rub the swordfish all over with the olive oil. Grill until just cooked through, about 5 minutes per side. Transfer the swordfish to a rimmed ovenproof serving platter or shallow baking dish. Pour the marinade over the fish, then cover with foil and let marinate for 15 minutes. Preheat the broiler. Uncover the swordfish and run under the broiler for about 1 minute to reheat and lightly glaze the top.

seafood gumbo

My recipe for gumbo changes depending on what fresh seafood I can get my hands on that day. But here's what never changes: a thick mahogany roux. It's what gives gumbo its structure and robust flavor. Oh, and a little Crystal Hot Sauce and molasses. If you want to use chicken or andouille sausage, go for it. Just make sure you sear either (or both!) in a hot skillet first to get them golden brown before adding to the mix. If you're using fresh okra, chop and sear that, too! The searing eliminates the gooey liquid (which is the number one complaint about okra), and the result is crispy brown okra bits that are magical. If using frozen okra, you can add it right to the gumbo with your shrimp, crab, and fish. Serve the gumbo with rice and crusty French bread. ~ **Julie**

½ cup plus 1 tablespoon **canola oil**

½ pound fresh or frozen **okra**, cut into ½-inch rounds

¾ cup **all-purpose flour**

1 large **onion**, diced

1 **shallot**, finely chopped

4 **celery stalks**, diced

1 large **green bell pepper**, cored, seeded, and diced

1 **jalapeño**, chopped

6 **garlic cloves**, minced

2 **dried bay leaves**

1½ teaspoons **dried thyme**

1½ tablespoons **blackstrap molasses**

1½ tablespoons **soy sauce**

1½ tablespoons **sherry vinegar**

1 tablespoon **fish sauce**

1 tablespoon **kosher salt**

¾ teaspoon **ground white pepper**

1 teaspoon **paprika**

3 cups **seafood broth**

3 cups **vegetable broth**

1 pound **shrimp**, peeled and deveined

1 pound jumbo **lump crab meat**

½ pound **cod** or other **white fish fillet**, cut into 1-inch pieces

⅓ cup chopped **parsley**

3 **scallions**, sliced

Juice of 1 **lemon**

Freshly ground black pepper

1. If using fresh okra, heat 1 tablespoon oil over medium heat in a large pot. Cook the okra until the gooey liquid disappears, 10 to 15 minutes. Transfer to a bowl.

2. Heat ½ cup oil in the same pot over medium-high heat until very hot. Sprinkle in the flour, reduce the heat to medium low, and cook, whisking frequently, until the roux turns dark brown. This can take 35 minutes to 60 minutes depending on the cookware. Once the roux begins to darken, pay close attention and adjust the heat accordingly. It should be a deep caramel color.

3. Increase the heat to medium and add the onion, shallot, celery, bell pepper, and jalapeño. Cook until softened, about 8 minutes, stirring frequently. Stir in the garlic, bay leaves, and thyme and cook 1 minute. Add the molasses, soy sauce, vinegar, fish sauce, 1 tablespoon salt, the white pepper, and paprika. Stir to combine and cook for 2 minutes more.

4. While stirring, slowly pour in the broths. Bring to a boil, then reduce to a steady simmer over medium-low heat. Cook, stirring occasionally, until slightly thickened, 25 to 30 minutes. If using frozen okra, add it now and cook until tender, 8 to 10 minutes. If using fresh okra, stir it in along with the shrimp, crab meat, and cod, and cook until the shrimp turn pink, 3 to 5 minutes. Remove the pot from the heat and discard the bay leaves, then stir in the parsley, scallions, and lemon juice. Season with salt and pepper.

citrus baked fish

Often, when I get the request to make a light and healthy meal, I immediately want to fall asleep from the lack of inspiration. I get it. Baked fish can be the "elevator music" of meals: pleasant enough, but at the end of the day you're just killing time until something more exciting comes along.

(I'm going to pause here and let you in on a little secret I have learned about cookbook writing. One of the formulas for creating these introductory headnotes is to write about what the common perception of a dish is and then follow it up with what you have done to make it more interesting. Another go-to is to talk about what the dish meant to you growing up. I hated fish as a kid, so I couldn't use that trick. There it is. The secret is out of the bag. You can write your own cookbook now. Okay, back to the recipe.)

Well, this baked fish is not only light and healthy but also just so happens to pack an exciting punch.

Brightly vibrant with citrus and a slather of peppery watercress pesto, garlic, and parsley, this has become my favorite way to effortlessly whip up a quick, delicious, and yes, healthy meal. ~ **Jesse**

⅓ cup **olive oil**, plus more as needed

Finely grated zest and juice of 1 **lime**

Finely grated zest and juice of 1 **lemon**, plus some slices for garnish

1 teaspoon **Dijon mustard**

1½ teaspoons **red wine vinegar**

2 **garlic cloves**

1 bunch of **watercress**, tough stems trimmed (about 2 cups)

2 **scallions**, white and green parts, roughly chopped

¼ cup **fresh parsley leaves**

Kosher salt and **freshly ground pepper**

4 (6-ounce) firm **white fish fillets** (such as tilapia, striped bass, or catfish)

Flaky sea salt

1. Preheat the oven to 350°F. Lightly grease a 9 by 13-inch baking dish with a little olive oil.

2. In the bowl of a food processor, combine the lime and lemon zests and juices, the mustard, vinegar, garlic, half the watercress, the scallions, parsley, ⅓ cup olive oil, and a generous pinch of kosher salt and pepper. Pulse until everything is finely minced and emulsified, 45 to 60 seconds. Season to taste with more salt and pepper.

3. Season the fish fillets on both sides with salt and pepper. Drizzle a little of the watercress pesto on the bottom of the baking dish. Place the fillets on top and then drizzle the remaining pesto evenly over everything. Bake until the fish is opaque and flakes apart when nudged with a fork, 15 to 20 minutes.

4. Chop the remaining watercress, then sprinkle over the baked fish and add a generous pinch of flaky sea salt. Serve immediately with lemon slices.

meatless mondays (for every day of the week)

At least once a month, Julie's husband tells her that he could be a vegetarian. Will occasionally feels bad about being a carnivore, and he was the one who suggested we have this "vegetarian" chapter. However, every time he sampled one of these dishes, he said, "Woah, that's delicious. You know what would be good? If you added some chicken to it or something. Wouldn't it be good with chicken?" The short answer is yes, but only because these recipes are such winners without it. If you are like us, these may just become your new favorite dishes—until we meat again!

coconut curry with crispy tofu

asparagus & leek galette

A galette is basically a lazy, half-assed pie, and Julie and I *love* them for that. Especially this savory version. We made this for a brunch once, and the reaction we got from our friends was as if we had just walked off the James Beard Award stage having won "Chef of the Decade."

I've always had a complicated relationship with piecrust. I can't relive it, but if you are in the mood for some casual masochism, the therapy session is documented in our pie curse—sorry, piecrust—instructions on page 208. Then, as you'll see on that page, Julie taught me a surefire way to make the perfect piecrust. Now I can't be stopped! This crust is a slightly more savory variation of our master piecrust recipe.

Oh, and in case you were wondering, the James Beard Awards are basically the Oscars of the culinary community. I've actually hosted the ceremony twice. "Chef of the Decade," though, isn't an actual category.

~Jesse

CRUST
- ⅔ cup **all-purpose flour**
- ⅔ cup **whole wheat flour**
- ½ teaspoon **kosher salt**
- ½ teaspoon **sugar**
- ½ cup (1 stick) **unsalted butter**, cut into ½-inch dice and chilled in freezer for at least 20 minutes
- 4 to 5 tablespoons **ice water**

FILLING
- 1 tablespoon **olive oil**
- 2 **leeks**, white and light green parts only, cut in half lengthwise, then sliced into ½-inch half-moons (see page 134)
- 1 bunch **asparagus**, tough ends trimmed, spears cut into 1-inch pieces (about 2 cups)
- **Kosher salt** and **freshly ground black pepper**
- ¾ cup **crème fraîche**
- ½ cup crumbled **feta cheese**
- 1 teaspoon finely grated **lemon zest**
- Juice of 1 **lemon**
- 1 tablespoon chopped **fresh tarragon**

ASSEMBLY
- 1 large **egg yolk**, beaten with 1 tablespoon water
- **Flaky sea salt**
- **Toasted sesame** or **benne seeds**

1. Make the crust: Preheat the oven to 400°F. Line a baking sheet with parchment paper.

2. In the bowl of a food processor, pulse together the flours, salt, and sugar until combined. Add the cold butter and pulse about 15 times, until the butter is broken down into pea-sized pieces. Add 4 tablespoons of the ice water, 1 tablespoon at a time, pulsing a few times between each addition. Continue to pulse until the dough just begins to come together, adding another tablespoon of water, 1 teaspoon at a time, if necessary. The mixture may look dry at first, but keep pulsing and the flour will hydrate. Dump the dough onto a piece of plastic wrap and shape into a 5-inch disc. Wrap the dough in the plastic wrap and place in the freezer for about 10 minutes. (If not using immediately, store the dough in the refrigerator for up to 3 days, until ready to use.) Wipe out the food processor.

3. Make the filling: Heat the olive oil in a medium cast-iron skillet or frying pan over medium heat. When the oil is shimmering, add the leeks and sauté, stirring occasionally,

recipe continues . . .

until softened, about 4 minutes. Add the asparagus and sauté until firm-tender, another 2 to 3 minutes. Season with salt and pepper. Remove the pan from the heat and let cool.

1. Add the crème fraîche, feta, and lemon zest and juice to the bowl of the food processor. Blend until smooth. Add the tarragon and pulse until incorporated. Season to taste with salt and pepper.

5. Assemble the galette: On a floured surface, roll out the dough into a 12-inch round, about ⅛ inch thick. Transfer to the baking sheet. Spread the creamy feta mixture over the center of the dough, leaving a 1-inch border all the way around. Arrange the cooled asparagus and leeks on top. Fold the edges of the crust over the filling, overlapping slightly; you want about 1 inch or so of the crust folded over, with the rest of the filling exposed. Brush the edges of the crust with the egg wash, then sprinkle with a little flaky salt and some sesame seeds. Bake until the crust is golden brown, 40 to 45 minutes. Remove from the oven and let stand 5 minutes before slicing and serving.

how to clean leeks

Julie here, reminding you to clean your leeks! You know how it is when you get home from a day at the beach and you find sand in areas you never knew existed? Well, that's kinda the same deal with leeks. The beautiful white and light green parts of the plant are that faint color because they are grown under the soil (blanched) until they are harvested, and since they are part of the onion family, they have delicate layers that trap soil.

This is how I taught Jesse how to clean leeks: First, trim off the tough, dark green part of the leaves and the root end. Then, slice the leek in half lengthwise and cut the 2 halves into 1-inch-long half-moons. Drop the sliced leeks into a clean sink or large bowl filled with cold water. Swish the leeks around and separate them to remove any dirt stuck between the layers. Use your hands to lift the leeks out of the water and place them in a clean, dry bowl. If the leeks are fresh from the ground and extra dirty, repeat this step once (or twice) more until all the dirt is gone. Spread the leeks out on a clean kitchen towel to dry. It's okay if they are still a little wet when it is time to use them.

miso polenta

Eating a mushroom is, for me, like going to the opera: I think I'm going to hate it, and then—once I'm experiencing it—it's pretty amazing. The key is maximizing the mushrooms' flavor, and this recipe does that brilliantly by infusing them with shallots, garlic, rosemary, thyme, and red wine. The miso brings umami to the polenta, and the polenta adds creaminess to the mushrooms.

There are a variety of misos available: white, yellow, red, black. White miso is the sweetest and mildest of the bunch. If you want an earthier and deeper flavor, substitute a darker miso. These mushrooms are robust enough to take it! Pro tip: If you have extra left over, lie to your guests and say that it is gone, hide it, and reheat it the next morning with a runny egg over it. You deserve it. They can make their own. ~ Julie

POLENTA

1 tablespoon **olive oil**

2 **garlic cloves**, minced

2 tablespoons **white miso**

4 cups **vegetable broth**, plus more as needed

1 cup **polenta**

Kosher salt and **freshly ground black pepper**

3 tablespoons **unsalted butter**

MUSHROOMS

¼ cup **grapeseed** or **olive oil**

1 pound **fresh mushrooms** (such as maitake), trimmed and torn into bite-size clusters

Kosher salt and **freshly ground black pepper**

1 medium **white onion**, cut in half and sliced into ¼-inch half-moons

2 **garlic cloves**, minced

1 teaspoon minced **fresh thyme**

1½ tablespoons **sherry vinegar**

½ cup **vegetable broth**

Chopped **fresh parsley**

Freshly grated **Parmesan cheese**

1. Make the polenta: Heat the olive oil in a large saucepan over medium heat. Add the garlic and cook until fragrant, 1 minute. Add the miso and 1 cup of the broth and whisk until the miso dissolves, another minute. Pour in the remaining 3 cups broth and bring to a simmer, then whisk in the polenta. Season with a big pinch each of salt and pepper. Reduce the heat to low and cook, uncovered, maintaining a slow simmer and stirring often, until the polenta is pudding-thick and the grains are tender, about 40 minutes. Add more broth or water, ¼ cup at a time, during the cooking process if the polenta gets too thick. Stir in the butter, and season to taste with salt and pepper. Cover and keep warm.

2. Make the mushrooms: Heat the oil in a large skillet over medium-high heat until shimmering. Add the mushrooms and season with salt and pepper. Cook, stirring occasionally, until the mushrooms start to release their liquid, about 4 minutes. Add the onion, garlic, and thyme and continue cooking until the mushrooms have browned and the onion is softened, another 10 minutes. Pour in the vinegar and broth and cook until most of the liquid has evaporated, 3 to 4 minutes.

3. Divide the polenta among shallow bowls, top with the mushroom mixture, and garnish with the parsley and Parmesan cheese. Serve hot or warm.

pop's pinto beans & cheddar cornbread

I admit it. I was a late bloomer to this Southern classic. This is my dad's favorite way to eat pinto beans. It also happens to be his favorite way to eat cornbread. The beans are so simple; simmered with a few aromatics, they make their own broth, and the cornbread is perfect for sopping up that broth. It wasn't until I became an adult that I really fell in love with my dad's favorite meal. (The day I realized that, I absolutely had an "OMG, I'm turning into my parents" meltdown. Next thing you know, I'll be subscribing to *Reader's Digest*, watching CSPAN, and wearing socks with sandals.)

Now, I need to get serious. True Southern cornbread calls for coarse cornmeal and no sugar, and this is coming from a girl who loves her sugar. Jesse, who is constantly asking me if I really *need* the sugar, did a victory lap around the kitchen when I told him I created a recipe without any. ∼ Julie

1 pound **dried pinto beans**

1 large **onion**, cut in half, one half finely chopped

1 (4-ounce) can diced **Hatch green chiles**, drained

3 **garlic cloves**, smashed

Hot water, as needed

2 teaspoons **kosher salt**, plus more as needed

Freshly ground black pepper

Sour cream

Cheddar Cornbread (recipe follows)

1. Rinse the beans under cool running water. Pick through them as you rinse and discard any bad-looking or shriveled beans. Transfer the beans to a large, deep pot or Dutch oven and cover with a couple of inches of cool water. Skim off any skins that float to the top. Soak the beans for at least 6 hours and as long as overnight. Drain the beans and rinse gently.

2. Return the beans to the pot and cover with clean, cool water by about 2 inches. Add the onion half, the chiles, and garlic. Bring to a boil over high heat, then reduce the heat to low. Partially cover the pot and gently simmer, stirring occasionally, for 45 minutes, until the beans are barely tender. Add hot water as needed to keep the beans submerged.

3. Stir in the 2 teaspoons salt and some pepper and continue simmering the beans for 45 minutes, until tender. Season to taste with more salt and pepper. Garnish with the chopped onion and the sour cream, and serve with the cornbread.

cheddar cornbread

MAKES ONE 9-INCH ROUND

2 tablespoons **grapeseed** or **canola oil**

2 cups **yellow cornmeal**

½ teaspoon **baking soda**

1¼ teaspoons **kosher salt**

2 cups **buttermilk**

2 large **eggs**

4 tablespoons (½ stick) **unsalted butter**, melted

1 cup shredded **cheddar cheese** (about 4 ounces)

1. Pour the oil into a 9-inch cast-iron skillet and swirl it around so it coats the entire bottom and up the sides. Place the skillet in the oven and preheat the oven to 400°F.

2. In a medium bowl, whisk together the cornmeal, baking soda, and salt. In another medium bowl or large liquid measuring cup, whisk together the buttermilk, eggs, melted butter, and shredded cheese. Add the buttermilk mixture to the cornmeal mixture and use a wooden spoon or rubber spatula to stir until just combined.

3. Carefully remove the skillet from the oven and pour in the batter. It will sizzle. Return the skillet to the oven and bake the cornbread until golden brown and a toothpick inserted in the center comes out clean, 20 to 25 minutes.

4. Carefully invert the pan onto a cutting board or plate, slice the cornbread, and serve hot or warm.

cheesy cauliflower enchiladas

At the end of the day, a typical vegetarian enchilada is really just a cheese enchilada, and we feel like we deserve more than that. The cauliflower here truly elevates the dish and makes it a hearty meal.

Mole is one of the most decadent sauces in Mexican cuisine; there are lots of versions, but this one is based on a smooth combination of chiles, nuts, cocoa, and spices. Our friend Chef Enrique Olvera created a mole at his Mexico City restaurant Pujol that he continued to tweak and modify for more than a thousand days! We understand that the average home cook doesn't have a thousand days of free time and wants to complete this dish in just one day, so we are hoping this eighty-five-minute mole fits better into your schedule. You can absolutely make the sauce a few days ahead of time, as it will keep in the refrigerator for three to five days, but we imagine you'll devour it way before then. We love this mole so much we also made it the star player in our Roasted & Smashed Sweet Potatoes (page 167).

~Jesse

MOLE SAUCE

- 2 ounces (10 to 12) dried mild to medium **chiles** (such as guajillos, New Mexico chiles, pasillas, or anchos), stemmed and seeds removed
- ¼ cup chopped raw **pecans**
- ¼ cup chopped raw slivered **almonds**
- ⅓ cup **sesame seeds**
- 1 teaspoon **coriander seeds**
- 1½ teaspoons **anise seeds**, or 1 teaspoon ground anise
- 1 teaspoon **cumin seeds**
- 2 **garlic cloves**
- 2¾ cups **vegetable broth**
- ½ cup **tomato puree**
- ⅓ cup unsweetened **cocoa powder**
- 2 tablespoons **honey**
- ½ teaspoon **ground cinnamon**
- ¼ teaspoon **ground allspice**
- 1 teaspoon **dried Mexican oregano** (see Note, page 140)
- 2 teaspoons **kosher salt**, plus more as needed
- 1 teaspoon **freshly ground black pepper**, plus more as needed
- 1 medium **onion**, halved with root end left intact, outermost layer removed
- 5 tablespoons **unsalted butter**

ENCHILADAS

- 1 medium head of **cauliflower** (about 1½ pounds)
- 3 tablespoons **olive oil**
- 1 teaspoon **kosher salt**
- ½ teaspoon **freshly ground black pepper**
- 1 cup grated **Monterey jack cheese** (about 4 ounces)
- 1 cup grated **cheddar cheese** (about 4 ounces)
- **Grapeseed** or **canola oil**, for greasing
- 8 (6-inch) **corn tortillas**
- 1 to 2 tablespoons **sesame seeds**
- **Sour cream** (optional)

1. Make the mole: Add the chiles to a large, heavy-bottomed pot and pour in enough water to just cover them (3 to 4 cups). Bring to a boil, then turn off the heat and cover the pot. Steep the chiles for 15 to 20 minutes (but not any longer, or they might become bitter). Drain and reserve ¼ cup of the soaking water if you prefer a spicier mole. Add the chiles to a blender or food processor.

recipe continues . . .

2. Wipe out the pot and heat over medium heat. Add the pecans, almonds, and the sesame, coriander, anise, and cumin seeds. Cook, stirring frequently, until toasty and fragrant, 3 to 4 minutes.

3. Transfer the nuts and seeds to the blender with the chiles and add the garlic, broth, tomato puree, cocoa powder, honey, cinnamon, allspice, oregano, 2 teaspoons salt, and 1 teaspoon pepper. Blend until smooth with a consistency slightly thinner than ketchup. Taste and adjust seasoning with more salt and pepper. If you want more heat, add some of the reserved chile liquid.

4. Pour the sauce back into the pot, add the onion and butter, and simmer gently, uncovered, over low heat, stirring occasionally, until the sauce has thickened slightly and darkened in color, 35 to 40 minutes. Remove the onion and discard. (You should have about 3½ cups of sauce.)

5. Make the enchiladas: Preheat the oven to 400°F. Line a baking sheet with foil.

6. Cut the cauliflower into ½-inch pieces. In a large bowl, toss the cauliflower florets with the olive oil, salt, and pepper.

Spread in an even layer on the baking sheet and roast until tender, 18 to 20 minutes. Place the cauliflower back in the bowl. Add ¼ cup of the mole sauce, half the Monterey jack, and half the cheddar. Use a flexible spatula to fold everything until well combined.

7. Spread enough mole sauce (¾ cup to 1 cup) to thinly cover the bottom of a 9 by 13-inch baking dish.

8. Brush a little bit of oil on a large pan or griddle, and heat over medium heat until just shimmering. Working a few at a time, add the tortillas and warm them, flipping occasionally, until they soften

and become slightly toasty, about 1 minute. Add more oil as needed.

9. Spoon a mound of the cauliflower filling (⅓ to ½ cup) onto the center of a tortilla and roll it up tightly. Place seam side down in the baking dish. Repeat with the remaining tortillas and filling. Spread the remaining mole (about 2 cups) on top of the enchiladas. Sprinkle the remaining cheese on top of the enchiladas and sprinkle the sesame seeds on top. Bake the enchiladas until the cheese is melted and bubbly, about 15 minutes. Serve hot, with a dollop of sour cream on top, if desired.

mexican oregano

You will see Mexican oregano called for a few times in our Southwest-influenced dishes, but it may be new for you. What is the difference between dried Mexican oregano and the dried oregano you probably already have in your spice rack? A lot, actually! The more common oregano that most people know is a Mediterranean variety and is from that part of the world (Italy, Greece, Morocco, Turkey). In fact, some spice distributors even label it as "Mediterranean Oregano." Mexican oregano is not only from a completely different region but also from an entirely different species and family of plant. It boasts an earthier, deeper, more woodsy flavor that allows it to shine through in the spicier and more robust Southwestern dishes. Are they interchangeable? That kinda depends on your palate. I actually keep Mexican oregano in my pantry as my default herb because I like the depth of flavor it brings to a dish, but if I am in a pinch and can't find some in the store, Mediterranean oregano absolutely does the trick.

coconut curry

SERVES 4

WITH CRISPY TOFU

Being friends with author and TV host Padma Lakshmi has its benefits. She'll say, "Pack your knives and go" whenever you ask her to; she knows how to throw a mean dinner party; and she has great Tom Colicchio stories. But one of the best things about our friendship is how much she's educated me about Indian food. She taught me the joy of cooking with coconut milk, and she opened me up to a world of spices, like star anise and cardamom pods. (Once, while she was staying at my house, she sleuthfully took stock of my spice drawer and mailed a box of items that she felt I was missing. #SneakyPadma.) Another thing Detective Lakshmi taught me was the significant difference between Thai curry and Indian curry. This curry, with its crispy tofu and bright lemongrass, is decidedly Thai-inspired.

Tofu is loaded with water, so squeezing it all out is key to getting a nice, firm texture. Rolling the tofu cubes in cornstarch helps them crisp up. (Warning! This crispy tofu is addictive. I've been known to snack on all these delicious nuggets before finishing the curry!) ~ Jesse

- 1 (14-ounce) package **firm tofu**
- **Kosher salt** and **freshly ground black pepper**
- ⅓ cup **cornstarch**
- 4 tablespoons **grapeseed** or **canola oil**
- 1 (14-ounce) can **full-fat coconut milk**
- 1 cup **vegetable broth**
- 1 tablespoon **soy sauce** or **coconut aminos**
- Finely grated zest of ½ **lime**
- 1 small **onion**, chopped
- 4 **garlic cloves**, minced
- 1 (2-inch) piece of **fresh ginger**, grated
- 1 **red bell pepper**, cored, seeded, and cut into 1-inch pieces
- 4 ounces fresh **sugar snap peas**, trimmed and cut into 1-inch pieces (about 1 cup)
- 3 ounces fresh **cremini mushrooms**, stemmed and sliced (about 1 cup)
- 1 stalk of **lemongrass**, tough outer layer removed, light and white parts finely chopped
- 1½ tablespoons **green curry paste** (such as Thai Kitchen Green Curry)
- ¼ teaspoon **ground coriander**
- ¼ teaspoon **ground cumin**
- 2 teaspoons **coconut sugar**, or 1 teaspoon **granulated sugar**
- Juice of 1 **lime**
- **Cooked rice**, warmed
- Chopped **fresh basil** or **cilantro**
- **Lime wedges**

1. Remove the tofu from its packaging and drain the liquid. Line a shallow dish with a few layers of paper towels and place the tofu on top. Set a plate on top of the tofu and weight it down with something heavy, like a cast-iron pan. Press the tofu for about 30 minutes. You may need to change the paper towels a couple times. Discard the paper towels.

2. Cut the tofu into 1-inch cubes. Season liberally with salt and pepper. Sprinkle the cornstarch all over the tofu and use your hands to evenly coat each piece.

3. In a large, heavy-bottomed pot or deep skillet, heat 2 tablespoons of oil over medium-high heat until the oil is hot and shimmering. Add the tofu in a single layer and cook, turning occasionally, until golden brown and crispy on all sides, 10 to 12 minutes. Line the dish you used for pressing

recipe continues . . .

the tofu with dry paper towels, then transfer the crispy tofu to the dish.

4. In a large liquid measuring cup or medium bowl, whisk together the coconut milk, broth, soy sauce, and lime zest.

5. Heat the remaining 2 tablespoons oil over medium heat in the same pot. Add the onion, garlic, and ginger and sauté until the onion has softened, 2 to 3 minutes.

Add the bell pepper, peas, mushrooms, and lemongrass and cook, stirring, until the vegetables soften, about 5 minutes. Add the curry paste, coriander, cumin, coconut sugar, and lime juice and cook, stirring, for 2 more minutes, until the vegetables are well coated. Season to taste with salt and pepper.

6. Pour in the coconut milk mixture, bring to a boil, then

reduce the heat to medium low and simmer, uncovered, stirring occasionally, until the liquid has reduced slightly, about 15 minutes.

7. Add the crispy tofu back to the curry, and season to taste with more salt and pepper. To serve, ladle the curry over rice and garnish with the basil or cilantro. Serve with lime wedges alongside.

FERIA DE S|
18 al 22 de ABRI|
LIT. ANEL - GRANAD|

tomato confit pasta

People who tell you "The best things in life take time" are annoying, but if they are talking about pasta sauce, they are also unfortunately correct. Luckily, this recipe is so easy you won't even notice the time going by. Tomato confit is one of those incredibly useful items that you can make ahead and break out for so many different occasions. After a nice, slow roast, the tomatoes get wrinkly and super concentrated with their own flavor, as well as that of the garlic and herbs and olive oil. Tomato confit also boasts the benefit of being incredibly easy to make. Toss all the ingredients into a pan, walk away, and enjoy the fringe benefits of fragrant roasting tomatoes and garlic that will fill your kitchen. The unpretentiousness of this delicious pasta dish is proof that you can be complex and simple at the same time. ～Julie

TOMATO CONFIT

1½ pounds **grape** or **cherry tomatoes**

6 **garlic cloves**

1½ teaspoons **kosher salt**

½ teaspoon **freshly ground black pepper**

1 teaspoon **sugar**

2 teaspoons **fresh thyme leaves**

1 sprig of **fresh oregano**

1 **dried bay leaf**

¾ cup **olive oil**

PASTA

Kosher salt

1 pound **short pasta** (such as penne or rigatoni)

3 **garlic cloves**, minced

1 medium **shallot**, finely chopped

½ teaspoon **ground cumin**

¾ cup **tomato sauce**

Freshly ground black pepper

½ cup **buttermilk**, room temperature

½ cup **heavy cream**, room temperature

1 tablespoon finely chopped **fresh oregano**

1. Preheat the oven to 275°F.

2. Make the confit: In a 9 by 13-inch baking dish, combine the tomatoes, garlic, salt, pepper, sugar, thyme, oregano, bay leaf, and olive oil. Toss to coat the tomatoes in the oil, then spread out in a single layer. They should fit snugly in the pan. Bake until the tomatoes are wrinkled and fragrant, shaking the pan a few times during cooking, about 1 hour 45 minutes. Let the tomatoes cool in the baking dish, then transfer them to an airtight container and pour the oil and herbs over the top. (The tomato confit will keep in the refrigerator for about 1 week or in the freezer for up to 6 months.)

3. Make the pasta: Bring a large pot of salted water to a boil. Cook the pasta until al dente, 2 to 3 minutes less than what the package instructs. Reserve 1 cup of the cooking water and drain the pasta. Toss the pasta with 1 tablespoon of the oil from the tomato confit to keep it from sticking together.

4. Heat 3 tablespoons of the confit oil in a Dutch oven or large, deep pot over medium heat. When the oil is shimmering, add the garlic, shallot, and cumin and cook until soft and fragrant, 1 to 2 minutes. Stir in the tomato sauce and 2 cups of the tomato confit (drained of excess oil). Season with salt and pepper. Add the pasta and reserved cup of cooking water. Cook until warmed through and the sauce is bubbling, about 2 minutes.

5. Stir in the buttermilk, cream, and oregano and cook until just warmed through and the pasta is well coated with the creamy sauce, 2 to 3 minutes more. Season to taste with more salt and pepper. Serve immediately.

ratatouille

Anyone who has taken even just a day of French knows that *ratatouille* means "delicious coarse vegetable stew." Ironically, *Coarse Vegetable Stew* was the original title of a certain Disney movie about a rat who longs to be a chef. That's a little bit of film history wrapped up in a French lesson for you. What I *also* know is that ratatouille translates to one of my family's favorite vegetarian meals. My kids love their ratatouille over pasta (with cheese), Will likes his mixed with rice, and I always put mine on a thick piece of baguette. It's also perfect completely on its own. Yes, the addition of okra here offers a bit of Southern flair, but it also helps to thicken the stew while supplying another layer of deep flavor. *Zut Alors!* This vegetable stew could win first place at the country fair! ~ Julie

⅓ cup **extra-virgin olive oil**

2 tablespoons **Italian seasoning** or **herbes de Provence**

½ teaspoon **celery seeds**

6 **garlic cloves**, smashed

2 large **onion**s, roughly chopped

1 **dried bay leaf**

1 medium **zucchini**, halved lengthwise and cut into 2-inch pieces

2 medium **yellow squash**, halved lengthwise and cut into 2-inch pieces

1 (10-ounce) package frozen sliced **okra**; or 10 ounces fresh okra, trimmed and cut into 2-inch pieces

3 jarred **roasted red peppers**, drained and cut into 2-inch pieces

1 large **globe (American) eggplant** (about 14 ounces), stem trimmed, quartered lengthwise, and cut into 2-inch pieces

1 (28-ounce) can **whole peeled tomatoes**

Kosher salt and **freshly ground black pepper**

Torn fresh **basil leaves**

Chopped **fresh parsley**

1. Preheat the oven to 400°F. Position a rack in the lower third of the oven.

2. Heat the oil in a large, deep pot or Dutch oven set over medium heat. When the oil is shimmering, stir in the seasoning, celery seeds, garlic, onions, and bay leaf. Cover the pot and cook, stirring occasionally, until the onions are just turning soft and everything is fragrant, about 10 minutes.

3. Stir in the zucchini, squash, okra, roasted peppers, eggplant, and tomatoes and season generously with salt and pepper. Transfer to the oven and cook, stirring occasionally, until the vegetables are tender and lightly browned, about 1½ hours. Season to taste with more salt and pepper. Fish out the bay leaf, then garnish with the basil and parsley, and serve warm with a crusty baguette or over rice or noodles, as desired.

shepherd's pie

I've always thought shepherd's pie was such a strange name because I considered shepherds as sort of babysitters of livestock. So it threw me that their pies were filled with ground lamb or beef. It's good I never owned a farm. I obviously know nothing about shepherds or livestock. Here, we have a shepherd's pie for a shepherd who babysits root vegetables and mushrooms. I do wonder how this shepherd feels about rutabaga, though, because that is one ugly root. If you can't picture what a rutabaga looks like, that's because it is usually hidden away in a corner of the produce section so as to not scare the people reaching for golden beets or tricolored heirloom carrots. But like most mysterious and misunderstood things, rutabagas have a lot to offer if you just give them a chance. Yes, we are burying it under mashed potatoes and mixing it with beautiful friends, but it still bravely and boldly contributes to this shepherd's pie. ~ Jesse

MASHED POTATO TOPPING

- 2 pounds **Yukon Gold potatoes**, peeled and quartered (about 6 medium)
- 1 tablespoon plus 1 teaspoon **kosher salt**
- ½ cup **whole milk**, warmed
- 4 tablespoons (½ stick) **unsalted butter**, softened
- ¼ cup grated **Gruyère** or **fontina cheese** (about 1 ounce)
- 2 large **egg yolks**

VEGETABLE FILLING

- 4 tablespoons (½ stick) **unsalted butter** or **neutral oil** (such as grapeseed or canola)
- 1 large **shallot**, finely chopped
- 2 **garlic cloves**, minced
- 1 medium **rutabaga** (about 10 ounces), peeled and cut into ½-inch dice
- 2 large **carrots**, cut into ½-inch dice
- Kosher salt
- 12 ounces mixed **fresh mushrooms** (such as portobello, shiitake, king oyster, and/ or cremini), roughly chopped
- 2 tablespoons **white miso paste**
- 1 tablespoon **tomato paste**
- 2 tablespoons **all-purpose flour**
- 1¾ cups **vegetable broth**
- 2 (15-ounce) cans **cannellini beans**, drained and rinsed, or 3½ cups **Creamy Butter Beans** (page 184)
- 2 teaspoons finely chopped **fresh thyme**
- ⅓ cup finely chopped **fresh parsley**
- 1½ teaspoons **lemon juice**
- Freshly ground black pepper

1. **Make the topping:** Add the potatoes and 1 tablespoon salt to a medium pot. Cover with cold water by 1 inch, bring to a boil, and cook until the potatoes are tender and easily pierced with a knife, 15 to 20 minutes. Drain the potatoes, then return to the pot. Mash the potatoes, then stir in the warm milk, butter, cheese, and remaining teaspoon salt. Allow the mixture to cool slightly, then stir in the egg yolks until thoroughly combined. Cover and keep warm while you make the filling.

2. Preheat the oven to 375°F.

3. **Make the filling:** In a Dutch oven or heavy pot, melt the butter over medium heat. Add the shallot and garlic and cook until soft, 2 minutes. Add the rutabaga and carrots and a generous pinch of salt and cook until just beginning to turn tender but still firm, 6 to 7 minutes. Stir in the mushrooms and cook until they begin to soften and their juices have evaporated, about 12 minutes. Stir in the miso paste and tomato paste and cook until well combined, another 2 to 3 minutes. Sprinkle the flour over everything and cook for 1 minute, stirring to coat the vegetables. Add the broth and beans and cook, stirring, until the mixture has thickened and is not too soupy, 3 to 4 minutes. Stir in the thyme, parsley, and lemon juice. Season to taste with salt and pepper.

4. Transfer the filling to a 9 by 13-inch baking dish (or leave in the Dutch oven), and spread in an even layer with a rubber spatula. Dollop the potatoes on top and use an offset spatula to spread in an even layer all the way to the edges to seal in the filling. Make fancy swoops on top, if desired. Bake until the potato topping begins to turn golden brown and the edges are bubbling, about 30 minutes. Let stand at room temperature for 15 minutes before serving.

gram's corn chowder

I have many of my Gram Edna's old recipes on perfectly typed index cards. (Her doing, not mine.) It had been years since I made Gram's Corn Chowder, and Julie and I started laughing when we began reading the ingredient list. It was like an inventory of the canned soup aisle in the grocery store. Cream of Mushroom! Cream of Corn! Cream of Cheddar Cheese! We didn't even know that last one existed. "Yes, good afternoon, I would like a large bowl of your finest cheese soup, please."

We took this chowder on as a challenge. I wanted to make our version vegetarian, so I had to physically carry Julie away from the eight strips of bacon Gram had in her original recipe. (Although, feel free to add it back in if you want! I know Julie will!) We also got rid of (most) of the canned soups. We left a can of creamed corn in . . . as an honor to my gram! ~Jesse

2 tablespoons **unsalted butter** or **olive oil**

1 medium **onion**, finely diced

1 **green bell pepper**, cored, seeded, and diced

2 **garlic cloves**, minced

1 teaspoon **ground fennel**

1 teaspoon **ground coriander**

1 teaspoon **kosher salt**, plus more as needed

¼ cup **all-purpose flour**

6 cups **vegetable** or **chicken broth**

1 large **russet potato**, peeled and cut into ½-inch dice

2 cups fresh or frozen **corn kernels**

1 (14.75-ounce) can **creamed corn**

½ cup **heavy cream**

Freshly ground black pepper

Minced **fresh chives**

1. In a heavy-bottomed pot, melt the butter over medium heat until hot and bubbly.

2. Add the onion, bell pepper, garlic, fennel, coriander, and 1 teaspoon salt. Cook over medium heat until the vegetables have softened, about 5 minutes. Add the flour and cook, stirring constantly, until the vegetables are coated and the flour is golden brown and toasted, about 3 minutes. Slowly add the broth, stirring to prevent lumps from forming. Add the potato and corn. Bring to a simmer over medium-high heat, then reduce the heat to medium low and cook until the potato is tender, 8 to 10 minutes more. Stir in the creamed corn and cream. Season to taste with salt and pepper.

3. Ladle into bowls and top with the chives.

taco
break

pulled-chicken tacos

SERVES
4 TO 6

WITH NEW
MEXICAN RED
CHILE SAUCE

I am obsessed with all things chile, but red chile sauce holds a special place in my heart. In fact, in an epic experimentation failure, I once tried to create a bloody Mary mix with canned enchilada red sauce. What can I say? The red chile is my favorite muse.

This recipe is a much more successful and practical use of New Mexico's famous export. We should take a moment to acknowledge that I am also a successful, practical, and famous New Mexican export, according to the *Albuquerque Journal*; "saucy" and "tender" are two adjectives the *Journal* used to describe my acting skills, and that describes this dish, too. Chicken is the wildly versatile building block for so many such meals. The cook time here is on the long side, but the preparation couldn't be easier. I like to batch-cook a few pounds of this delicious meat and freeze it in portions until I need it; that way it's

ready to go at a moment's notice. My favorite night to make this shredded chicken is Tuesday, because it's Taco Tuesday—and also that's when *The Voice* airs.

~Jesse

PULLED CHICKEN
2 pounds boneless, skinless **chicken thighs**
Kosher salt and **freshly ground black pepper**
2 tablespoons **olive oil**
1 large or 2 small **onion**s, cut in half and thinly sliced into half-moons
2 **garlic cloves**, minced
1 tablespoon **dried oregano**

1 teaspoon **ground cumin**
2 cups **New Mexican Red Chile Sauce** (page 67)
½ cup **chicken broth**, plus more as needed

ASSEMBLY
12 **corn tortillas**
2 **avocados**, peeled and sliced
1 cup **sour cream**

1. **Make the chicken:** Preheat the oven to 350°F. Arrange a rack in the lower third of the oven.

2. Season the chicken on both sides with salt and pepper.

3. Heat the olive oil in a Dutch oven or large, heavy oven-safe pot over medium heat until shimmering. Add the onion, season with a pinch of salt, and sauté until starting to soften, 6 to 7 minutes. Add the garlic,

oregano, and cumin and cook until fragrant, about 1 minute.

4. Add the chicken, the chile sauce, and ½ cup broth and stir to combine. The sauce should cover the chicken; if not, add more chicken stock. Put on the lid and bake until the chicken is very tender, 2 hours.

5. Use two forks to shred the chicken in the sauce. Taste and adjust seasoning as needed.

6. **Assemble the tacos:** To heat the tortillas, either microwave a small stack wrapped in damp paper towels, or toast individual tortillas for a few seconds each in a dry skillet over medium heat until soft and hot, removing to stack on a plate. Cover with a clean dish towel to keep warm. Spoon the chicken and a bit of sauce onto the tortillas. Top with the avocado and sour cream. Serve at once.

ground beef & pickle tacos

SERVES
4

One of the California restaurants we really miss is Malo. The East Side of L.A. hasn't been the same since they shut their doors. They were known for their vibrant vibe, 2-for-1 margarita happy hour, and extensive taco menu. But the star of the place was always the ground beef and pickle taco. It was like the secret love child of a hamburger and a taco. Not that either of us knows anything about having secret love children, but if we did, we'd name it Malo because we really do miss that place. We hope our loving homage to this unexpected combo makes you as happy as it makes us. ~ J&J

BEEF AND PICKLE

2 tablespoons **grapeseed** or **canola oil**

1 medium **onion**, diced

3 **garlic cloves**, minced

1 pound 80/20 or 85/15 **ground beef** (see Note)

¼ teaspoon **ground cinnamon**

2 teaspoons **ground paprika**

2 teaspoons **ground cumin**

1 teaspoon **chipotle chile powder**

2 teaspoons **dried Mexican oregano** (see Note, page 140)

1 teaspoon **kosher salt**

½ teaspoon **freshly ground black pepper**

¼ cup crushed **canned tomatoes**

1 (4-ounce) can diced **Hatch green chiles**

⅓ cup diced **dill pickles**, plus more for topping

⅓ cup **pickle juice**

ASSEMBLY

8 hard **taco shells**

Shredded **cheddar cheese**

Shredded **lettuce**

Sour cream

1. **Make the beef and pickle:** Heat the oil in a large skillet over medium heat. Add ¾ cup of the diced onion and the garlic and sauté until softened, about 4 minutes. Add the ground beef, cinnamon, paprika, cumin, chile powder, oregano, salt, and pepper and cook until the beef is no longer pink, about 8 minutes.

2. Add the tomatoes, chiles, pickles, and pickle juice. Reduce the heat to medium

low and cook, stirring occasionally, until the juices thicken and the flavors have melded, 15 to 20 minutes.

3. **Assemble the tacos:** Spoon the ground beef mixture into taco shells and sprinkle with shredded cheese, shredded lettuce, the remaining ¼ cup diced onion, and some more diced pickle. Top with the sour cream and serve 2 tacos per person.

beef ratios

When you see numbers on a label for ground beef, it usually means the lean-to-fat ratio. So, 85/15 is 85 percent lean to 15 percent fat, which is a pretty lean, meaty mix. Another common choice, 70/30, is usually about as high in fat as most blends will go, and is a good option for juicy burgers.

beer-battered catfish tacos

WITH MEYER
LEMON TARTAR
SAUCE

Walk into any diner in the South and you will find on the menu fried catfish served with greens and tartar sauce. Walk up to any taco stand in the Southwest and you will find fish tacos. Walk into my backyard and you will find a Meyer lemon tree. Now run, don't walk, to the corner of South and Southwest and make this delectable and tangy beer-battered catfish taco with a tartar sauce spiked with Meyer lemon.

Meyer lemons are slightly sweeter and less acidic than regular lemons. No Meyer lemons on hand? No problem. Substitute with a mix of fresh lemon and orange zest and juice. Or you can just use regular lemons. It will still be delicious! ~Julie

Grapeseed or canola oil
Kosher salt
1 teaspoon **garlic powder**
1 cup **all-purpose flour**
½ cup medium-grind **yellow cornmeal**
½ cup **cornstarch**
12 ounces **dark beer** (such as Modelo Negra)
1 large **egg**
1 pound boneless, skinless **catfish fillets** (or other firm white fish, like tilapia, red snapper, or striped bass), cut into 1 by 3-inch strips

ASSEMBLY
4 or 8 **corn tortillas**
Meyer Lemon Tartar Sauce (recipe follows)
Thinly sliced **watermelon radishes**
Shredded **green cabbage**
Chopped **fresh cilantro leaves**
Meyer lemon wedges, for serving

1. **Make the catfish:** Preheat the oven to 200°F or the "warm" setting, if you have that. Set a wire rack over a baking sheet. Pour enough oil into a large, heavy-bottomed cast-iron skillet with high sides or Dutch oven to reach a depth of about 2 inches, making sure you still have a couple inches of clearance. Heat the oil over medium-low heat until the temperature reaches 350°F. (Use a thermometer.)

2. In a medium bowl, whisk together the salt, garlic powder, ¾ cup of the flour, the cornmeal, and cornstarch. Add the beer and egg and whisk until a mostly smooth batter

forms. Place the remaining ¼ cup flour in a separate shallow bowl or plate.

3. Season the catfish pieces with some salt. Lightly dredge the pieces in the flour, shaking off any excess. Dip the fish in the beer batter and shake or wipe off any excess. Working in batches to avoid overcrowding the pan, fry the fish in the hot oil for about 4 minutes, flipping once, until golden brown. Increase the heat to medium high to reach or maintain the 350°F.

4. As the fish is finished frying, transfer the pieces to the rack and sprinkle with some

more salt. Place in the oven to keep warm while you fry the remaining fish.

5. **Assemble the tacos:** To heat the tortillas, either microwave a small stack wrapped in damp paper towels, or toast individual tortillas for a few seconds each in a dry skillet over medium heat until soft and hot, removing to stack on a plate.

6. Distribute the fish pieces among the tortillas and top with some of the tartar sauce, then add the radishes, cabbage, and cilantro. Serve with Meyer lemon wedges alongside for squeezing over the tacos.

meyer lemon tartar sauce

MAKES ABOUT ¾ CUP

½ cup **mayonnaise**

1 teaspoon **white wine vinegar**

1 teaspoon chopped **fresh dill**

1 teaspoon finely grated **shallot**

1 teaspoon finely grated **Meyer lemon zest**

1 tablespoon fresh **Meyer lemon juice**

1 teaspoon **Crystal Hot Sauce**

Kosher salt and **freshly ground black pepper**

In a medium bowl, whisk together the mayonnaise, vinegar, dill, shallot, lemon zest and juice, and hot sauce. Season to taste with salt and pepper. Cover the bowl with plastic wrap and refrigerate until ready to use.

serve
with

———

"Is there something I can bring?" is *the* most commonly asked question your guests will have before a dinner party. And if you are like us, you always reply with "Just yourselves!" But what you're really thinking is: *You can also bring a positive attitude, and that sweater you borrowed from me last fall, and a side dish of literally anything. Figure it out on your own. Why do I have to manage you? I have a chicken to roast!* Might we suggest buying a copy of this book for your friends and dog-earing this page for them?

$$$$ Creamed Collards

roasted cauliflower

We know, cauliflower can sometimes be a snooze; that's where gremolata comes in. What's gremolata, you ask? It's a condiment usually made from finely chopped herbs, garlic, and citrus. There are many variations on this zesty, bright garnish, and ours incorporates fried capers, which add a flavor bomb of umami. Now, like the quiet guy in high school who suddenly dates the homecoming queen, your cauliflower has become cool—all because of the gremolata (which, funny enough, was the name of my high school's homecoming queen). ~**Jesse**

1 large head of **cauliflower** (about 2 pounds), cut into florets

10 tablespoons **olive oil**

Kosher salt and **freshly ground black pepper**

2 cups grapeseed or **canola oil**

6 tablespoons **olive oil**

1 teaspoon finely grated **orange zest**

¼ cup **orange juice**

1 teaspoon finely grated **lemon zest**

1 teaspoon **lemon juice**

⅓ cup finely chopped **scallions**, white and light green parts only (about 3 **scallions**)

¼ cup finely chopped **fresh parsley**

1 teaspoon **paprika**

Red pepper flakes (optional)

⅔ cup **capers**, drained and patted dry

4 **garlic cloves**, chopped

⅔ cup **pine nuts**

1. Preheat the oven to 400°F. Line a rimmed baking sheet or sheet pan with aluminum foil.

2. Toss the cauliflower on the baking sheet with 4 tablespoons (¼ cup) of the olive oil and a large pinch of salt and pepper. Spread in an even layer and roast for about 30 minutes, until golden brown and slightly tender but not mushy.

3. Meanwhile, line a plate with paper towels. In a small saucepan, heat the grapeseed oil over medium heat until it reaches 350°F.

4. In a large bowl, whisk together the remaining 6 tablespoons olive oil, the orange zest and juice, lemon zest and juice, scallions, parsley, paprika, 1 teaspoon salt, and red pepper flakes, if using.

5. When the oil is hot, add the capers and garlic and fry until the capers begin to burst open and the garlic turns golden brown, about 4 minutes. Use a slotted spoon to transfer the capers and garlic to the paper towel–lined plate to drain. Add the pine nuts to the hot oil and fry, stirring occasionally, until golden brown, 1 minute.

6. Add the fried capers, garlic, and pine nuts to the gremolata and gently stir to combine. Add the cauliflower and toss to coat. Season to taste with more salt and pepper.

caramelized green beans

Trimming green beans always reminds me of my grandmother. Yes, my memory involves a front porch, a rocking chair, and a bucket into which we would toss the trimmed beans. Listen, I'm just as shocked as you are that my green bean memory is basically a Norman Rockwell painting. I refuse to call it cliché, however. What can be a cliché is the classic bean preparation: salt, pepper, butter, lemon . . . I'm getting drowsy just writing this. We wanted to enliven these beans by caramelizing them a bit and then giving them a jolt of excitement from aromatic garlic, ginger, and shallot. We wanted to f**k them up without f**king with them too much. Sorry, Granny, for cursing. ~ Julie

3 tablespoons **unsalted butter**

1½ pounds **green beans**, stem ends trimmed

3 **garlic cloves**, smashed

1 (1-inch) piece of **ginger**, peeled and halved

1 small **shallot**, halved

½ teaspoon **dried dill**

Kosher salt and **freshly ground black pepper**

¾ teaspoon **sugar**

Finely grated zest and juice of ½ **lemon**

1. In a large stainless-steel or cast-iron skillet, melt the butter over medium heat until bubbling. Add the green beans and toss well to coat. Add the garlic, ginger, shallot, and dill and season with a big pinch of salt and pepper. Reduce the heat to medium low and cook the green beans, tossing frequently, until darkened in color, slightly wilted, and caramelized, 35 to 40 minutes. Some beans will be darker and softer than others; that's okay.

2. Sprinkle in the sugar and cook for another minute to dissolve. Remove the pan from the heat and stir in the lemon zest and juice. Season to taste with more salt and pepper.

tammy's party squash

SUMMER SQUASH CASSEROLE WITH BUTTERY RYE BREAD CRUMBS

Who's Tammy? That's a great question. I don't know. Tammy's Party Squash is a recipe I found in the cookbook *Treasures from Heaven*, a collection of recipes by women of the First United Methodist Church of Cullman, Alabama. It's the type of cookbook that's meant to stay within a community and not expected to make the *New York Times* bestseller list—at least I don't think so. But now it proudly lives on my kitchen countertop next to actual *New York Times* bestsellers, and when I'm homesick, it's my cure-all. Tammy, wherever you are, if you happen to find yourself with a copy of this cookbook, know that you inspired this casserole. And I have some questions.* In hopes of one day meeting you, we decided to keep your name in the title. We also felt that "Julie's Tammy's Party Squash" would be a bit too much. ~Julie

*Tammy, did you actually take this dish to parties? Do you and your friends throw down when you make it? Is there a party in your mouth when you eat it, or is it just a blast to make? I mean, who doesn't love a party squash?!

Nonstick cooking spray

3 tablespoons **canola** or **grapeseed oil**

3 pounds medium-large **yellow squash** (about 4), cut into ¼-inch-thick rounds

2 tablespoons **unsalted butter**

1 medium **onion**, chopped

1 **green bell pepper**, cored, seeded, and chopped

2 teaspoons **kosher salt**, plus more as needed

1 teaspoon **freshly ground black pepper**, plus more as needed

3 **garlic cloves**, minced

½ teaspoon **caraway seeds**

¼ teaspoon **dried dill**

¼ teaspoon **red pepper flakes** (optional)

2 tablespoons **water**

2 large **eggs**

¾ cup **sour cream**

2 cups grated **fontina cheese** or **cheddar** (8 ounces)

3 cups **Rye Bread Crumbs** (recipe follows)

1. Preheat the oven to 350°F. Lightly coat a 9 by 13-inch baking dish with nonstick spray.

2. Heat the oil in a large skillet over medium-high heat. When hot and shimmery, add the squash. Cook, stirring often, until tender and lightly browned, about 25 minutes. Drain the squash in a colander.

3. Wipe out the skillet and melt the butter over medium heat. Add the onion, bell pepper, 1 teaspoon of the salt, and the 1 teaspoon pepper. Cook until softened, about 10 minutes. Add the garlic, caraway, dill, and red pepper flakes, if using, and cook until fragrant, 30 seconds. Add the water and cook until evaporated, 1 to 2 minutes. Remove the pan from the heat and stir in the squash, mashing some of the squash as you stir it in. Season with the remaining teaspoon of salt and more pepper as desired.

4. In a small bowl, whisk together the eggs and sour cream until smooth. Add to the squash, along with 1 cup of the grated cheese, and stir to incorporate. Transfer the squash mixture to the baking dish, smooth the top, then sprinkle on the remaining 1 cup cheese. Top with the bread crumbs.

5. Bake until squash is dark golden brown and bubbly around the edges, 25 to 30 minutes. If the bread crumbs are browning too quickly, cover the dish with foil. Let cool for about 5 minutes before serving.

rye bread crumbs

MAKES ABOUT 3 CUPS

3 tablespoons **unsalted butter**

3 or 4 slices of **stale rye bread**, crumbled (3 cups)

Kosher salt and **freshly ground black pepper**

Melt the butter in a large skillet set over medium heat. When the butter is hot and foamy, add the bread crumbs and toss to coat. Cook, stirring occasionally, until toasty and browned, about 8 minutes. Season to taste with a pinch of salt and pepper, then transfer to a large plate to cool.

charred brussels sprouts

Like most kids who grew up eating Brussels sprouts, I truly hated them. My mom would boil them or steam them, and they would taste like tiny cabbages, which I suppose they are. It wasn't until the Brussels sprouts boom of the early 2000s that I reconsidered my stance; it seemed like every hip restaurant was suddenly serving them. The first Brussels sprouts that I truly loved was at David Chang's Momofuku. They were deep-fried and covered in fish sauce, which took the sprouts in a completely different direction, one that almost made it taste like a french fry. Here, we simulate that effect, only we roast the sprouts to a crispness and give them a hit of buttery acid with this truly bomb vinaigrette. I feel like I just dated myself with that last sentence. ~Jesse

BRUSSELS SPROUTS

3 tablespoons **olive oil**

1½ pounds **Brussels sprouts**, trimmed and cut in half lengthwise

Kosher salt and **freshly ground black pepper**

BROWN BUTTER VINAIGRETTE

2 tablespoons **red wine vinegar**

1 tablespoon **extra-virgin olive oil**

1 tablespoon chopped **shallot**

½ tablespoon finely chopped **fresh thyme**

½ teaspoon **sugar**

Kosher salt and **freshly ground black pepper**

6 tablespoons **Brown Butter** (page 263), melted

1. Make the sprouts: Preheat the oven to 400°F.

2. Heat the olive oil in a large cast-iron skillet over medium heat until shimmering. Add the sprouts, cut side down, in a single layer. Cook, undisturbed, until the sprouts begin to brown on the bottom, about 5 minutes. Season with salt and pepper, give the pan a few shakes to move the sprouts around, then transfer the pan to the oven. Roast until the sprouts are darker in color and tender, about 10 minutes.

3. Make the vinaigrette: Add the vinegar, olive oil, shallot, thyme, sugar, a big pinch of salt and pepper, and the brown butter to a glass jar. Cover with the lid and shake vigorously to emulsify.

4. Pour the vinaigrette over the sprouts and toss to coat. Season to taste with more salt and pepper.

roasted & smashed sweet potatoes

It bothers us when vegetarians get short shrift at dinner parties. Who has been to events where the meat eaters get huge portions of roast beef and the vegetarians get just a slab of cauliflower that is being called "steak"? This dish offers everyone at the table—vegetarians and meat eaters alike—something that's (pardon our French) f**king delicious. Mole is a super-complex Mexican sauce, whose most well-known version is based on toasted chiles, seeds, nuts, and sometimes chocolate, that can oftentimes be intimidating. We have developed a version that is fairly easy to master. The bonus here is that the mole can also be used in our Cheesy Cauliflower Enchiladas (page 139). Score two for the vegetarians! ~ J&J

2 tablespoons **olive oil**, plus more as needed

2 large **sweet potatoes**

¾ cup **mole sauce** (see page 139)

Sour cream or **crema**

Honey

1. Preheat the oven to 400°F. Line a baking sheet with foil and lightly grease the foil with a little olive oil.

2. Pierce the sweet potatoes all over with a fork and rub with 1 tablespoon of the olive oil. Place on the baking sheet and roast until tender and easily pierced with a fork, about 45 minutes. Remove the potatoes from the oven and let cool for about 10 minutes.

3. Using the bottom of a spatula, or your hand if you're tough, gently flatten each sweet potato to about 1 inch thick. Don't worry if some of the flesh escapes; just scoop everything back together with the spatula.

4. Heat the remaining tablespoon olive oil in a large cast-iron skillet over medium heat. When the oil is shimmering, use the spatula to scoop the smashed sweet potatoes into the pan. Sear for about 2 minutes on each side, until crispy and brown. Transfer to a platter and drizzle with the mole. Serve warm with sour cream, and honey.

Roasted and Smashed Sweet Potato with Mole and Honey; Chermoula-Roasted Broccolini with Tahini Dressing; Charred Brussels Sprouts with Brown Butter Vinaigrette; Roasted Cauliflower with Fried Capers and Pine Nut Gremolata

south by southwest spoonbread

You can't spell "Southwest" without "South," and as Julie and I compare notes on the flavors of our childhoods, it's been fun to mash things up, as we do here with our take on spoonbread. What's spoonbread? Great question, reader. If cornbread is what you cut into squares and eat with your fingers, spoonbread is . . . well, the name says it all. Custard-like, spoonbread is cornbread's more decadent older sister, like the Zsa Zsa to cornbread's Eva Gabor. Here, we bring in the Southwest with the red and green bell peppers, jalapeño, garlic, and sage. So get out your fanciest spoon and go to town, Zsa Zsa style; you'll love it, dahling. ~Jesse

3 tablespoons **unsalted butter**, plus more as needed

1 medium **onion**, finely chopped

1 **red** or **orange bell pepper**, cored, seeded, and finely chopped

1 **green bell pepper**, cored, seeded, and finely chopped

1 **jalapeño**, seeded and minced

2 teaspoons **kosher salt**

2 **garlic cloves**, minced

1 teaspoon chopped **fresh sage**

1 teaspoon chopped **fresh chives**

3 cups **whole milk**

1 cup **water**

1 cup fine- or medium-ground **yellow cornmeal**

2 teaspoons **baking powder**

3 large **eggs**, room temperature

1. Preheat the oven to 350°F. Generously grease a 9-inch baking dish or oval gratin dish with a little butter.

2. In a medium saucepan, melt the 3 tablespoons butter over medium heat. Add the onion, bell peppers, jalapeño, and salt. Cook until soft, 5 to 7 minutes. Add the garlic, sage, and chives and cook until fragrant, about 1 minute. Add the milk and water and bring to a simmer. While whisking continuously, pour in the cornmeal in a slow, steady stream. Continue whisking, over medium heat, until the cornmeal has absorbed all the liquid and the mixture is thick and smooth, about 2 minutes. Remove the pan from the heat and stir in the baking powder. Let cool for about 5 minutes, stirring often to prevent clumping.

3. Add the eggs to a liquid measuring cup or medium bowl. Use a handheld electric mixer to whisk the eggs at medium speed until foamy and the color has lightened some. Pour one-third of the beaten eggs into the batter and stir to incorporate. Add another third and stir again. Add the remaining eggs and stir well. Transfer the batter to the baking dish. Bake until the top feels dry to the touch and a toothpick inserted into the center comes out slightly clean, 20 to 25 minutes. Serve warm, straight from the dish.

chermoula–roasted broccolini

Fooling your kids is a necessary part of being an adult, from pretending there is a Santa Claus to calling wine "mommy juice." This dish is a great way to trick your kids into eating their vegetables. Chermoula is a bold and herby Moroccan sauce that has become our secret weapon in the kitchen, while the tahini dressing brings a nutty richness to the roasted broccolini. (Side note: Jesse told me that if he ever does drag, his drag name will absolutely be "Nutty Richness." Don't try to take it; he has already claimed it.)

By the way, if this is the first you are hearing about Santa Claus, we apologize. We are sorry you had to find out this way—in a broccolini recipe. ~Julie

BROCCOLINI
Olive oil, for greasing
2 bunches broccolini (about 12 ounces total), tough ends trimmed, or 1 large broccoli crown, cut into florets
Kosher salt

CHERMOULA
1 cup fresh cilantro leaves and tender stems
1 cup fresh parsley leaves
¼ cup fresh mint leaves
2 garlic cloves
½ teaspoon ground cumin
½ teaspoon smoked paprika
½ teaspoon kosher salt, plus more as needed
1 teaspoon finely grated lemon zest
Juice of 1 lemon
½ teaspoon red pepper flakes
½ cup olive oil

TAHINI DRESSING
¼ cup tahini
1 teaspoon finely grated lemon zest
Juice of 1 lemon
¼ teaspoon smoked paprika
Kosher salt
¼ cup boiling water

GARNISH
1 to 2 tablespoons sesame seeds
Red pepper flakes

1. Preheat the oven to 350°F. Lightly grease a baking sheet with a little olive oil.

2. Place the broccolini or broccoli florets on the baking sheet and season with a pinch of salt.

3. Make the chermoula: Add the cilantro, parsley, mint, garlic, cumin, paprika, ½ teaspoon salt, the lemon zest and juice, red pepper flakes, and olive oil to a food processor or blender. Pulse until the herbs are finely chopped and the sauce is smooth. Season to taste with more salt.

4. Pour the chermoula over the broccolini and toss to coat well, then arrange the broccolini in a single layer and roast until tender and starting to crisp, 20 to 25 minutes.

5. Make the tahini dressing: In a small bowl, whisk together the tahini, lemon zest and juice, paprika, and a pinch of salt until well combined and thick. Add the boiling water, 2 tablespoons at a time, until the sauce is smooth and pourable. Season to taste with more salt.

6. Transfer the roasted broccolini to a serving platter, drizzle the tahini dressing over the top, and garnish with the sesame seeds and more red pepper flakes, if desired.

hatch green chile mac & cheese

My good friend Lea DeLaria, whom I met in 1997 doing the Broadway revival of *On the Town*, has a story about me baking a mac and cheese casserole without boiling the macaroni first, thinking that would make the top crispy. I swear this never happened, but she tells the story so often that even I'm starting to believe it is true. Thankfully, I've worked through my pasta neuroses with Julie, and together we have developed a creamy stovetop mac and cheese that marries her go-to version with my first love—spicy and slightly sweet Hatch green chiles. There's no crispy top here, but if you do want one, just be sure to boil the macaroni first or Lea's going to make fun of you, too. ~**Jesse**

Kosher salt

1 pound **elbow macaroni** or other short pasta

2 teaspoons **grapeseed** or **canola oil**

4 tablespoons (½ stick) **unsalted butter**

1 large **shallot**, finely chopped (about ⅓ cup)

1 small **onion**, finely chopped (½ cup)

6 **garlic cloves**, minced

2 tablespoons minced **jalapeño**

¼ cup **all-purpose flour**

4 cups **whole milk**, warmed

2 cups freshly grated **Monterey jack cheese** (8 ounces)

½ cup freshly grated **pepper jack cheese** (2 ounces)

3 (4-ounce) cans diced **Hatch green chiles**, drained

1 teaspoon **dried Mexican oregano** (See Note, page 140)

Freshly ground black pepper

1. Bring a large pot of salted water to a boil. Add the pasta and cook until al dente, 7 to 9 minutes. Drain, transfer to a large bowl, and toss with a couple of teaspoons oil, to keep the noodles from sticking.

2. In a large saucepan, melt the butter over medium heat. Add the shallot, onion, garlic, and jalapeño and cook, stirring, until softened, about 3 minutes. Stir in the flour and cook until toasty, about 2 minutes.

3. Switching to a whisk, slowly pour in the warm milk, whisking constantly. Bring to a simmer and cook, stirring frequently, until the sauce begins to thicken, 3 to 5 minutes. Add the cheeses in two additions and stir until melted; the sauce will start to thicken to the consistency of queso.

4. Remove the pan from the heat and stir in the green chiles, oregano, a pinch of salt, and some pepper. Add the pasta, stir until well coated, and serve.

$$$$
creamed
collards

It is Southern folklore that collards are said to bring you wealth if you make them on New Year's Day. Consider this a fiber-packed lottery ticket that just so happens to also be made with cream. I'm not sure eating collards on January 1 has worked for me, but I don't see the point of messing with fate. Creamed collards will always be a staple in my house on New Year's Day. ~ **Julie**

2 tablespoons **olive oil**

4 **garlic cloves**, minced

¼ cup **vegetable broth**, plus more as needed

3 bunches **collard greens, mustard greens**, or **lacinato kale** (about 2½ pounds total), thick stems removed and leaves torn into pieces

Kosher salt and **freshly ground black pepper**

½ cup **heavy cream**

½ cup (4 ounces) **cream cheese**, softened

½ teaspoon **paprika**

¼ teaspoon freshly grated **nutmeg**

Juice of 1 **lemon**

Grated **Parmesan cheese**

1. Heat the olive oil in a large skillet over medium heat until shimmering. Add the garlic and cook until fragrant, about 1 minute. Stir in the ¼ cup broth and add enough collards to fill the skillet. Stir until wilted, then add more greens, continuing until all have been added. Season with salt and pepper. Continue cooking until the greens have completely wilted and most of the liquid has evaporated, 7 to 8 minutes from the first addition of greens.

2. Heat the cream in the microwave or on the stovetop in a small saucepan until very hot. Whisk in the cream cheese, paprika, and nutmeg until smooth.

3. Pour the cream mixture into the greens and continue cooking until bubbly, about 4 minutes. Add the lemon juice and stir to incorporate. The greens should be creamy and loose but not runny; if they are too dry, add more broth or water, 1 tablespoon at a time. Season to taste with more salt and pepper. Transfer to a serving dish and sprinkle generously with grated Parmesan cheese.

note

If you plan on making the Grilled Swordfish in Potlikker Marinade on page 124, reserve about 1 cup of the potlikker (broth) from the braised greens before serving the greens. The potlikker will keep in an airtight container in the refrigerator for up to 5 days or for months in the freezer.

braised turnip greens

There was nothing fancy about my parents' wedding. They settled on December 28 as the date for tax purposes (smart move). My mom didn't want an engagement ring and she was content with a humble gold band. The ceremony took place at a small Southern Baptist church just outside of Hanceville, Alabama. The most dramatic event at the wedding was when Aunt Irma's baby knocked over the crystal punch bowl, which was full of foamy mint-green nonalcoholic sherbet punch. Four days later, my folks rang in the New Year with a low-budget dinner of turnip greens and black-eyed peas. Not yet quite full, my dad announced that he was "gonna have a little cornbread crumbled up in potlikker." My mom, hearing "pot of liquor," started to freak out, thinking she had just promised a lifetime to a man who couldn't even enjoy his cornbread without soaking it in booze. Only later did she learn that he wasn't talking about moonshine. Potlikker is the heavenly broth left over after cooking turnip greens or collards. The smoky ham hock, bitter greens, tart vinegar, and salty liquid create a magical potion. How my mom grew up a mere fifteen miles from my dad and never heard of potlikker still amazes me, but ironically it is now one of her favorite treats. ~Julie

2 tablespoons **unsalted butter**

2 tablespoons **grapeseed** or **canola oil**

4 **garlic cloves**, minced

1 small **onion**, diced

½ teaspoon **red pepper flakes**, plus more as needed

2 pounds **turnip greens** or other sturdy greens (such as collards or mustard greens), thick stems removed and leaves chopped or torn into 1- to 2-inch pieces

3 tablespoons **apple cider vinegar**

2 cups **chicken** or **vegetable broth**

1 cup **water**

1 tablespoon **sorghum syrup** or **brown sugar**

1 pound **smoked ham hock** (optional)

Kosher salt and **freshly ground black pepper**

1. In a large, heavy-bottomed pot, melt the butter and oil together over medium-high heat. Add the garlic and onion and sauté until the onion has softened and has a little color to it, about 5 minutes.

2. Add the ½ teaspoon red pepper flakes, then add the turnip greens, a few handfuls at a time, stirring between each addition to wilt slightly. Sauté until evenly wilted, 2 to 3 minutes more. Add the vinegar and cook for about 2 minutes, until almost evaporated.

3. Add the broth, water, sorghum syrup, and ham hock, if using, and stir to combine. Season with a pinch of salt and black pepper. Bring to a boil, then reduce the heat to medium low and bring to a simmer. Cover the pot and cook the greens, stirring occasionally, until very tender, about 1 hour.

4. Before serving, taste and adjust seasoning if needed with more salt and pepper.

spring pea soup

This soup is creamy in texture, but the only actual cream involved is the dollop you add as a finishing touch. The pea soup I grew up eating either was from a can or was made from dried split peas. Not here! This soup is made with the same package of peas I just used as a cold compress *on my aching hip*! That's right! We use the frozen kind. Not only are they inexpensive, but they are also consistently sweet and tender and heat through incredibly quickly, making it virtually unnecessary to thaw them first. I guess I have always found pea soup to be the Eeyore of soups, but here the white wine, garlic, soft herbs, and that dilly dollop of cream bring a bit of zip and elegance to the bowl. It's bouncy, trouncy, flouncy, pouncy, and fun, fun, fun, fun, fun! ~Jesse

SPRING PEA SOUP

- 3 tablespoons **unsalted butter**
- 1 large **onion**, diced
- 1 **celery stalk**, diced
- 2 **garlic cloves**, chopped
- 1 **star anise pod**
- 3 tablespoons **dry white wine**
- 2 cups **frozen peas**
- 4 cups **chicken** or **vegetable broth**
- 1½ teaspoons **kosher salt**, plus more as needed
- ½ cup **fresh parsley leaves and tender stems**, roughly chopped
- ½ cup **fresh basil leaves**, roughly chopped
- 2 tablespoons finely chopped **fresh chives**
- 4 sprigs of **fresh dill**, stems and fronds separated, fronds chopped

DILL CREAM

- 1 cup **sour cream**
- 1 **garlic clove**, finely grated on a Microplane
- 1 tablespoon finely chopped **fresh dill**
- 1 tablespoon **fresh lemon** or **lime juice**
- ¼ teaspoon **kosher salt**
- ¼ teaspoon **ground white pepper**

1. Make the soup: Melt the butter in a large saucepan or Dutch oven over medium heat. Add the onion, celery, garlic, and star anise and cook, stirring occasionally, until the onion is softened, 4 to 5 minutes. Add the wine and cook for 1 minute, until the strong alcohol scent has dissipated. Stir in the peas, broth, and 1½ teaspoons salt. Cover, increase the heat to medium high, and bring to a boil, stirring occasionally. Once boiling, reduce the heat to low and simmer, covered, until the peas are soft, 8 to 10 minutes.

2. Remove the star anise and discard. Add the parsley, basil, chives, and dill stems. Puree in a blender until smooth, leaving the top open a crack and holding it with a towel so the steam doesn't blow it off. Stir in the dill fronds. Season to taste with more salt.

3. Make the dill cream: In a small bowl, stir together the sour cream, garlic, dill, lemon juice, salt, and white pepper until smooth.

4. Ladle the warm soup into bowls and dollop with the dill cream.

butter bean & cauliflower soup

You have to know how hard this was for me, but I did it! I made a completely dairy-free soup! Where's my parade? My Southern soul needs to use an ingredient that at least sounds like a dairy product, though, so I present the butter bean! Velvety, creamy, and yes, buttery, this legume is actually just an albino lima bean. Full of protein and pureed smooth like a cream soup, this completely vegan dish gets an extra boost of pizazz with the herbaceous pistou. Basically a fancy, nut-free pesto, pistou is a great tool to have in your back pocket. (Although I have ruined a few pairs of jeans this way.) It's also delicious with a little Parmesan cheese. So, if you add the cheese, just disregard everything I said and cancel the parade.

~Julie

SOUP

3 tablespoons **olive oil**

1 medium **white onion**, chopped

2 **celery stalks**, chopped

1 small **fennel bulb**, trimmed, cored, and thinly sliced

2 **garlic cloves**, chopped

1 **dried bay leaf**

1 sprig of **fresh rosemary**

4 cups **chicken** or **vegetable broth**

1 medium head of **cauliflower** (about 1½ pounds), chopped into florets

2 cups **Creamy Butter Beans** (recipe follows), drained, or 1 (15-ounce) can **cannellini beans**, drained and rinsed

2 teaspoons **kosher salt**, plus more as needed

¼ teaspoon **ground white pepper**, plus more as needed

PISTOU

½ cup **fresh dill** or **fennel fronds**

½ cup **fresh parsley leaves and tender stems**

½ cup **fresh basil leaves**

1 **garlic clove**

Finely grated zest of 1 **lemon**

Juice of ½ **lemon**

⅓ cup good-quality **olive oil**

1 teaspoon **kosher salt**

¼ teaspoon **red pepper flakes** (optional)

1. **Make the soup:** In a large saucepan or Dutch oven, heat the olive oil over medium heat. When the oil is shimmering, add the onion, celery, fennel, garlic, bay leaf, and rosemary and sauté until the vegetables are soft and are just turning golden, about 8 minutes. Add the broth and cauliflower.

Increase the heat to medium high, cover, and simmer until the cauliflower is tender, about 10 minutes.

2. Add 1¼ cups of the butter beans, the salt, and the pepper, and simmer until the beans are warmed through. (Note that if you're using canned beans,

you'll have only about ¼ cup beans left for the topping; that's okay.) Remove the bay leaf and rosemary sprig. Carefully transfer the soup to a blender, working in batches if necessary, and puree until smooth. Season to taste with more salt and pepper. Cover to keep warm.

recipe continues . . .

3. Make the pistou: Add the dill, parsley, basil, and garlic to a food processor and pulse until finely chopped. Add the lemon zest, lemon juice, olive oil, salt, and red pepper flakes, if using, and pulse to combine. The pistou should be spoonable but still have some texture from the herbs.

4. Ladle the soup into bowls and swirl in the pistou. Top the bowls with some of the reserved beans, if desired.

creamy butter beans

MAKES 6 TO 7 CUPS

1 pound **dried butter beans**

1 **celery stalk**, halved crosswise

1 medium **white onion**, halved

1 **dried bay leaf**

1 smoked **ham hock** (optional; obviously makes the soup not vegan)

Kosher salt and **freshly ground black pepper**

Olive oil and **fresh herbs**, for serving (optional)

Rinse the beans and pick through for shriveled beans or stones. Add to a large, deep pot and cover with cool water. Soak at room temperature for at least 6 hours but ideally overnight. Drain the soaked beans and return to the pot. Cover with 2 inches of fresh, cool water. Add the celery, onion, bay leaf, and ham hock, if using. Bring to a boil over high heat, then reduce the heat to low, cover, and simmer until the beans are tender and creamy, 1 hour. Season to taste with salt and pepper. Remove the celery, onion, bay leaf, and ham hock and discard. Serve the beans in their broth with good-quality olive oil and some fresh herbs, or use them in this delicious soup.

roasted sweet potato soup

"Depth of flavor" is something you always hear when you are talking about really delicious soup. I prefer "wallop of gusto"—it has more zing. What *also* has zing is this perfect roasted sweet potato soup. The soup itself is like the first contestant you meet on the new season of *The Bachelorette*. Then the next two limos pull up and the Sorghum Butter and Peppery Cracklins swagger onto the scene with their flashy wallop of gusto, and the soup realizes, "Oh, damn! Game is *on*!" The best part of this ridiculous analogy is that in this scenario, we are all the Bachelorette. ~ Julie

- 2½ pounds **sweet potatoes** (about 4 large), peeled and chopped into 2-inch pieces
- 2 tablespoons **olive oil**
- 2 teaspoons **kosher salt**, plus more as needed
- ½ teaspoon **freshly ground black pepper**, plus more as needed
- 4 tablespoons (½ stick) **unsalted butter**
- 1 medium **onion**, chopped
- 2 **garlic cloves**, minced
- ½ teaspoon **ground cumin**
- ½ teaspoon **ground cinnamon**
- ½ teaspoon **ancho chile powder**
- 2 tablespoons **apple cider vinegar**
- 5 cups **chicken broth**
- ½ cup **heavy cream**, warmed
- ½ cup **whole milk**, warmed
- **Lemony Sorghum Brown Butter** (page 263)
- **Crispy Cracklins** (recipe follows)

1. Preheat the oven to 400°F. Position a rack in the center of the oven.

2. On a rimmed baking sheet or sheet pan, toss the sweet potatoes with the olive oil, 1 teaspoon of the salt, and ½ teaspoon of pepper. Spread in an even layer. Roast until tender and light golden brown, 25 to 30 minutes.

3. In a large saucepan or Dutch oven, melt the butter over medium-low heat. Add the onion and cook, stirring occasionally, until softened, 10 to 15 minutes. Stir in the garlic, cumin, cinnamon, and chile powder and cook until fragrant, about 2 minutes. Stir in the vinegar, broth, the roasted sweet potatoes, and remaining teaspoon salt. Increase the heat to medium high, bring to a boil, then reduce the heat to low and simmer for 5 minutes, or until the sweet potatoes are very tender and the flavors have melded.

4. Carefully transfer the soup to a blender and puree (in batches, if necessary) until very smooth. (Alternatively, for a smoother soup, strain through a fine-mesh sieve into a clean saucepan.) Add the cream and milk and season to taste with more salt and pepper. Ladle the soup into bowls, drizzle with a spoonful of brown butter, and top with the cracklins.

recipe continues . . .

crispy cracklins

I used to be a serious crispy-chicken-skin thief when I was young. (I'm still young, thank you very much, but I have reined in my habit.) One time, while my mom was busy setting the dinner table, I took the time to sneak into the kitchen and peel the crispy skin off of everyone else's chicken. I ate the evidence right away. Considering my mom was aware she did not just finish making *skinless* thighs, the jig was up pretty quickly. ~Julie

Skin from 4 large
chicken thighs
Kosher salt and **freshly ground black pepper**

1. Preheat the oven to 350°F. Line a baking sheet with parchment paper.

2. Dry the chicken skin well with paper towels. Place the pieces on the baking sheet and sprinkle with salt and pepper. Cover with another sheet of parchment paper, then place another baking sheet (or a cast-iron skillet—anything heavy) on top to keep the skins flat. Bake until the skins are golden and crispy, 25 to 30 minutes.

3. Chop the skins into bite-size pieces for soup or, if using on biscuits, leave them whole. I'm sure that this is going to be no surprise coming from the Great Chicken Skin Kleptomaniac, but cracklins are best eaten the same day, freshly cooked. However, if you want to make them ahead, store them in an airtight container for a few hours; you can re-crisp them a bit by warming them in the oven. But (and this is your last warning) I *will* eat them if you turn your back on me.

chicory salad & benne croutons

I always assumed that as I became an adult, I would grow to love anchovies—the way I grew to love gorgonzola cheese and bedtime. It just never happened. And yet, I love this salad. Am I in deep denial that this creamy vinaigrette is housing anchovies? I don't know. I'm changing the subject!

The costar of this hearty salad is the rustic benne croutons. Benne is an heirloom sesame-seed variety known for its deep flavor and slight bitterness. It is native to Africa and was brought to the South by the enslaved in the 1700s. I had never heard of this ingredient before Julie brought it to my attention, and now I love it so much I always have a bag on hand in my freezer. You can definitely find benne seeds online and in most specialty grocery stores, or you can use their more common cousin (we all have one), toasted sesame seeds. This dish is pretty substantial, so it works as both a side salad for a group and as a meal for a couple. Although I may have to rethink our marriage the day Justin asks if we can share a salad for dinner. ~ Jesse

BENNE CROUTONS
Nonstick cooking spray

1 large **egg white**

2 tablespoons **olive oil**

3 cups **stale bread cubes**, torn into ½- to 1-inch pieces

3 tablespoons **benne seeds** or **toasted sesame seeds**

2 teaspoons **flaky sea salt**

CREAMY ANCHOVY VINAIGRETTE
5 tablespoons **extra-virgin olive oil**

Juice of 2 **lemons**

2 tablespoons **sour cream**

1½ tablespoons **honey**

1½ tablespoons minced **anchovies** (from 4 to 5 fillets)

1 **garlic clove**, minced

Kosher salt and freshly ground black pepper

SALAD
5 ounces **mixed chicory** (such as endive, frisée, and/or radicchio), torn into bite-size pieces

5 ounces **fresh kale**, stems removed, leaves torn into bite-size pieces

1 cup **fresh parsley leaves**

1 **avocado**, diced

Kosher salt and freshly ground black pepper

Freshly grated **Parmesan cheese**

1. Make the croutons: Preheat the oven to 350°F. Line a baking sheet with parchment paper and lightly coat with nonstick spray.

2. In a large bowl, use an electric hand mixer to beat the egg white until soft peaks form, about 2 minutes. Slowly drizzle in the olive oil and continue beating until the mixture is creamy and emulsified. Fold in the bread cubes until well coated. Sprinkle in the benne seeds and flaky salt and mix until well incorporated. Spread the bread cubes in an even layer on the baking sheet. Bake, stirring halfway through, until toasty brown and crisp, 20 to 25 minutes.

3. Make the vinaigrette: Add the olive oil, lemon juice, sour cream, honey, anchovies, and garlic to a glass jar. Screw on the lid and shake vigorously to emulsify. Season to taste with salt and pepper. Store in the refrigerator until ready to use.

4. Assemble the salad: In a large bowl, massage the chicory and kale with half the vinaigrette. Fold in the parsley and avocado, and add the croutons. Add more vinaigrette and season to taste with salt and pepper. Sprinkle the salad with the Parmesan and serve.

fried green tomato salad

SERVES
4 TO 6

WITH
BUTTERMILK
VINAIGRETTE

There is great debate as to whether the idea of fried green tomatoes originated in the South or in the Midwest. What can't be disputed is that Fannie Flagg's best-selling book and hit movie named after that fried fruit is unmistakably set in Whistle Stop, Alabama. So I firmly believe that the South deserves full bragging rights here. Listen, if you turn your back on an ingredient while a Southerner is in the room, chances are we are gonna try and fry it. The natural tartness of the unripe green tomatoes mellows when they are cooked, and because unripe green tomatoes are firm, they're perfect for frying. Pairing the fried tomatoes with ripe tomatoes makes them shine even brighter, while the buttermilk dressing gives that final hit of tangy acidity that really makes this salad sing.

~Julie

BUTTERMILK VINAIGRETTE
½ cup **buttermilk**
2 tablespoons **mayonnaise**
Juice of ½ **lemon**
1 tablespoon **extra-virgin olive oil**
1 **garlic clove**, minced
1 teaspoon finely chopped **fresh oregano**
Pinch of **cayenne pepper** (optional)
Kosher salt and freshly **ground black pepper**

FRIED GREEN TOMATOES
⅔ cup **all-purpose flour**
1 teaspoon **kosher salt**

1 teaspoon **paprika**
¾ cup **buttermilk**
1 large **egg white**
¾ cup finely ground **yellow cornmeal**
2 unripe **tomatoes** (10 to 12 ounces total), sliced into ¼-inch-thick rounds
½ cup **canola oil**
Flaky sea salt

SALAD
2 cups **fresh arugula**
1½ cups ripe **cherry** or **grape tomatoes**
¼ medium **red onion**, thinly sliced
¼ cup **fresh oregano leaves**

1. Make the vinaigrette: In a medium bowl or resealable container, whisk together the buttermilk, mayonnaise, lemon juice, olive oil, garlic, oregano, and cayenne, if using. Season to taste with salt and pepper. Cover and store in the refrigerator until ready to use.

2. Make the tomatoes: In a shallow bowl or pie pan, whisk together ⅓ cup of the flour, the salt, and paprika. In another shallow bowl, whisk together the buttermilk and egg white. In a third shallow bowl, whisk together the remaining ⅓ cup

flour and the cornmeal. Set a wire rack inside a rimmed baking sheet lined with aluminum foil (for easy cleanup). Coat each tomato slice with the flour mixture, then dip into the buttermilk, then coat with the cornmeal mixture. Arrange the breaded tomato slices on the wire rack in a single layer.

3. Heat the oil in a large cast-iron skillet over medium-high heat until shimmering. You'll know the oil is ready if you sprinkle in a little flour and it sizzles immediately. Working in

batches to avoid overcrowding the pan, fry the tomato slices until golden brown, 2 to 3 minutes per side. Transfer the fried tomatoes back to the wire rack and sprinkle with the flaky sea salt.

4. Assemble the salad: Spread the arugula on a serving platter. Arrange the fried green tomatoes on top. Sprinkle the cherry tomatoes and onion slices over the fried tomatoes and garnish with the oregano. Drizzle on the dressing and serve.

Clockwise from top: Fried Green Tomato Salad; Grilled Chicken & Romaine with Alabama White BBQ Sauce; Chicory Salad with Benne Croutons

i love
olive salad

One of my most cherished acting opportunities was getting to originate the role of Leaf Coneybear in the Broadway musical *The 25th Annual Putnam County Spelling Bee*. My favorite line in the script comes when the character of Olive Ostrovsky tries to flirt with a fellow spelling bee contestant by saying that if you switch the first two vowels of her name, it spells "I love." Yes, I created this olive salad so that I could brag about my Broadway credentials in my first cookbook, but this is also one delicious salad! Buttery Castelvetrano olives are paired with hearts of palm, while the darker, winey saltiness of Kalamata olives features in the vinaigrette. Julie has turned me on to the brilliance of panko bread crumbs; toasted with a bit of Parmesan cheese, this crumble is the "bacon bits" of croutons. ~Jesse

KALAMATA OLIVE VINAIGRETTE

2 tablespoons minced **shallots**

2 tablespoons **red wine vinegar**

Juice of 1 **lemon**

½ cup **olive oil**

Kosher salt and **freshly ground black pepper**

¼ cup finely chopped **Kalamata olives**

SALAD

6 cups chopped **red leaf** and/or **romaine lettuce** (about 5 ounces)

1 cup **hearts of palm**, sliced into ½-inch coins and separated

1 cup pitted **Castelvetrano olives**, halved

1 cup **Parmesan Crumble** (recipe follows)

Kosher salt and **freshly ground black pepper**

1. **Make the vinaigrette:** Add the shallots, vinegar, lemon juice, olive oil, and salt and pepper to a glass jar. Screw on the lid and shake vigorously until the dressing is fully blended. Add the Kalamata olives and gently shake to incorporate.

2. **Make the salad:** In a large bowl, toss the lettuce with the hearts of palm and Castelvetrano olives. Add about two-thirds of the dressing and toss well to coat. Sprinkle with half the cheese crumble and toss. Season to taste with salt and pepper. Add more dressing and crumble, as desired.

parmesan crumble

MAKES 1 CUP

1 cup **panko bread crumbs**

½ cup grated **Parmesan cheese**

Kosher salt and **freshly ground black pepper**

In a large, dry skillet, toast the panko over medium-high heat, stirring frequently, until light golden, 3 to 4 minutes. Add the Parmesan and stir until the cheese melts and the mixture is golden brown and clumps a bit, about 1 minute more. Remove the pan from the heat and season to taste with salt and pepper. Let the crumble cool in the skillet, stirring occasionally.

grilled cabbage coleslaw

To some, coleslaw is always that underappreciated dish at a potluck that goes unnoticed or is just there to pile on your pulled-pork sandwich—which, by the way, is a necessary component of a pulled-pork sandwich. But you know who was paying attention to coleslaw? Me! Some like it creamy and mayonnaise-y; some (my dad) like it sweet and vinegary. I love all coleslaw, so with this recipe I feel I've accomplished satisfying everyone. The charring combined with the roasted peanut oil adds depth in a way that mayonnaise does, and the flavors play beautifully off the slightly sweet vinegar dressing. ~ Julie

PEANUT VINAIGRETTE

¼ cup **roasted peanut oil**

2 tablespoons **brown rice vinegar** or **apple cider vinegar**

Finely grated zest of ½ **lime**

Juice of 1 **lime**

1 tablespoon **soy sauce** or **liquid aminos**

1 **garlic clove**, grated on a Microplane

1 teaspoon **honey**

2 tablespoons chopped **fresh basil leaves**

1 **jalapeño**, seeded and finely chopped

Kosher salt and **freshly ground black pepper**

SLAW

1 medium head of **green cabbage**, quartered and cored

Olive oil

2 medium **carrots**, coarsely grated

2 **scallions**, white and green parts sliced on the diagonal to ¼-inch thickness

½ cup torn **fresh basil leaves**

Kosher salt and **freshly ground black pepper**

½ cup chopped **roasted peanuts**

1. **Make the vinaigrette:** In a glass jar, combine the peanut oil, vinegar, lime zest and juice, soy sauce, garlic, honey, basil, and jalapeño. Screw on the lid and shake well to combine. Season to taste with salt and pepper.

2. **Make the slaw:** Heat a grill, grill pan, or griddle to medium-high heat. Brush the cabbage quarters with olive oil and grill until well charred on all sides, 10 to 15 minutes total. Transfer to a cutting board and cover with aluminum foil. Let rest for 5 minutes.

3. Thinly slice the cabbage. Transfer to a large bowl, and add the carrots, scallions, and basil. Toss to combine. Drizzle the vinaigrette over the vegetables and toss again. Season to taste with salt and pepper. Serve warm or cold. Top with the roasted peanuts just before serving.

biscuits
~by Julie

My mom was a working woman, so I'm not ashamed to say that when she made biscuits, she often turned to the Pillsbury Doughboy for help. I'll always have a soft spot in my heart for the taste of canned biscuits and the joy I felt when I heard that popping sound of the can getting whacked on the edge of the counter.

Made-from-scratch buttermilk biscuits, on the other hand, were a special treat when I was growing up. I lived for the smell of toasting flour and melting butter filling our kitchen, and I still do today. After only three minutes of baking, I'll hear my kids yell, "I smell biscuits!" Then, without fail, everyone (including the dog) finds their way to the kitchen island and lingers around the stove.

A good biscuit is like a hot, steamy love affair among flour, butter, and salt. It's taken me a few years to develop my perfect biscuit—they are flaky, layered, and laminated with a lot of butter. Every Southern cook has his or her own methods. For instance, how to laminate the dough, or how many times the dough should be folded. These are small but impactful subtleties that make one biscuit so different from another. But the one golden rule that every biscuit maker agrees on is using a light touch—that is the ticket to a delicate, fluffy biscuit. Folding helps the dough come together and creates the layers, but too much folding and overworking the dough strengthens the gluten bonds and makes the biscuits tough and chewy.

Biscuits are versatile. The purist in me often wants just a warm buttery biscuit, straight from the oven. But if I'm feeling particularly hormonal and emotional, I want my biscuit stuffed with fried bologna, salted ham, or fried chicken. If I need a quick dessert for a dinner party, I'll make strawberry shortcakes using golden flaky biscuits piled high with strawberries and whipped cream, thereby charming the pants off my dinner guests. But my all-time favorite approach is a biscuit slathered with (even more) butter and drizzled with sorghum syrup. What's not to love?

buttermilk biscuits

MAKES ABOUT
12
BISCUITS

Unlike drop biscuits in which the dough just gets plopped onto the baking tray, these flaky buttermilk biscuits get their layers with a tiny bit more work. Round, square, or rectangular, the shape doesn't really matter as long as they are risin', which is exactly what you will be doing once you've tried these beauties!

4 cups **all-purpose flour**, plus more as needed

1 tablespoon **kosher salt**

2 teaspoons **granulated sugar**

2 tablespoons **baking powder**

1 cup (2 sticks) **unsalted butter**, cut into ½-inch dice and chilled in the freezer for at least 20 minutes; plus 2 tablespoons **unsalted butter**, melted

1¾ cups very cold **buttermilk**

Turbinado sugar or **sorghum** for finishing (optional)

1. In a large bowl, whisk together the flour, salt, granulated sugar, and baking powder. Add the cold butter and toss to coat. Use your fingers or a pastry cutter to pinch the butter into the flour, rubbing it between your fingers and thumbs until the mixture resembles coarse meal and a few pea-size pieces of butter remain. Drizzle in half the buttermilk and use your hands or a rubber spatula to fold the dough a few times. Drizzle in the remaining buttermilk and continue to fold the mixture until the dough just comes together, taking care not to overmix. The dough will be shaggy.

2. Lightly flour a clean work surface and turn out the dough onto it. Gather the dough into a scrappy ball and knead it a few times to incorporate all the dry and shaggy bits. Lightly flour a rolling pin and roll the dough out into a 1-inch-thick rectangle with rounded edges, about 9 by 13 inches. Fold the dough in thirds, bringing the top third down and the bottom third up and stacked on top, like a business letter. Turn the dough seam side down and rotate 90 degrees, then roll out again to a 1-inch-thick rectangle. This time it will look more like an even rectangle.

3. Repeat the folding, rotating, and rolling 3 more times, for a total of 4 folds, lightly flouring the surface and the rolling pin as needed to prevent sticking. After the final fold, gently roll the dough into an 8-inch square, about 1½ to 2 inches high. Wrap the dough tightly in plastic wrap and chill in the refrigerator for at least 30 minutes, or up to 3 days.

4. Preheat the oven to 375°F. Line two large baking sheets with aluminum foil.

5. Roll out the chilled dough to a ¾-inch thickness. Use a 3- or 3¼-inch round biscuit or cookie cutter to stamp out the biscuits, pressing the cutter straight down (don't twist!) to keep the flaky layers intact. Gather up the scraps and gently reshape. Roll out again to a ¾-inch thickness and stamp out more biscuits, repeating once more, if needed. You should have about 12 biscuits.

6. Place the biscuits on the baking sheets, spacing evenly. Generously brush the tops with the melted butter. Sprinkle with the turbinado sugar, if using (great for making strawberry shortcakes). Bake the biscuits until golden brown, 20 to 25 minutes. Serve as desired.

biscuits & cracked peppercorn gravy

My mom was usually in charge of driving me to school, but on the days she wasn't able to, I knew my morning commute would be a little more exciting because my dad would take a detour to Hardee's drive-thru for a "breakfast on the go." My order was always the same: a biscuit and gravy, and orange juice with a peel-back foil seal. These biscuits and gravy don't arrive quite as quickly, but they are still my favorite way to start a day! Note that if you're making enough gravy for a full batch of 12 biscuits, you can double or even triple this recipe.

5 tablespoons **all-purpose flour**

¼ teaspoon **garlic powder**

⅛ teaspoon **onion powder**

⅛ teaspoon **paprika**

⅛ teaspoon **ground white pepper**

½ teaspoon **freshly ground black pepper**, plus more as needed

5 tablespoons **fat of choice** (such as bacon, sausage, or schmaltz) or equal parts **unsalted butter** and **neutral oil**, such as canola oil

2¾ cups **whole milk**, plus more as needed

1 teaspoon **kosher salt**, plus more to taste

4 to 6 **Buttermilk Biscuits** (page 198)

Hot sauce of choice

1. In a small bowl, whisk together the flour, garlic powder, onion powder, paprika, white pepper, and black pepper.

2. Heat the fat in a large cast-iron skillet over medium heat until hot and bubbly. Sprinkle in the flour mixture and cook, stirring constantly, until toasty and fragrant, 2 minutes. Slowly drizzle in the 2¾ cups milk, whisking constantly. The mixture will initially seize up and thicken; continue slowly drizzling in milk and stirring until the mixture begins to thin again. Stir until smooth and until the gravy starts to bubble, about 1 minute. Remove the pan from the heat and stir in the 1 teaspoon salt. Add more milk if the gravy is too thick. Season to taste with more salt and black pepper.

3. Slice the biscuits in half and place the 2 halves open on individual plates. Spoon the gravy over both halves and sprinkle with hot sauce and more black pepper, if desired.

crispy cracklin biscuit sandwiches

When I was first at culinary school, one of the things I said aloud was "If I ever open a restaurant, I will have a crispy cracklin sandwich on the menu." Listen, I love a fried chicken and biscuit combo as much as anyone else, but my complaint has always been that fried chicken is such a bossy, flashy star (something I also once called Jesse) that it outshines its companion. The beauty of crisp chicken skin is that it's delicate enough not to overpower the biscuit while still providing a savory and salty crunchiness to the dish. How many biscuits you need for these sandwiches depends on how many biscuits you consider a single serving; one biscuit could be enough for one person, but if I'm coming over, I will want at least two.

Buttermilk Biscuits (page 198)

Crispy Cracklins (page 187)

Sorghum Butter (page 263) or **Lemony Sorghum Brown Butter** (page 263)

I probably don't need to spell this out, but here is what you do: Slice the biscuits in half and sandwich the cracklins in between. Drizzle either of the sorghum butters inside. Eat.

strawberry shortcakes with rhubarb cream

SERVES 4 TO 6

The rhubarb cream here was a happy accident. We had a bit of rhubarb left over after roasting some for a savory dish, so we mixed it into the whipped cream we were serving with dessert. Strawberry and rhubarb are a classic duo for pies, so I thought, *Why not for shortcakes as well?* Now I don't want them any other way! Strawberry shortcake will always be my husband's number one choice for dessert. I can pour an entire day into making a cake (which I did while testing our Old-Fashioned Yellow Cake, page 211), but if there are biscuits and cream around, he's going to opt for that instead. So, here you go, Will. I've written out the instructions for you. Let me know when you are finished making them, because I want one.

½ cup **sugar**

¼ cup **water**

1 to 2 large stalks **fresh rhubarb** (about 4 ounces), very thinly sliced (about 1 cup)

Pinch of **kosher salt**

1 cup **crème fraîche, sour cream,** or **full-fat Greek yogurt**

1 **vanilla bean**, seeds scraped, or 1 teaspoon **vanilla bean paste**

1½ pounds **fresh strawberries**, hulled and quartered (about 4½ cups)

4 to 6 **Buttermilk Biscuits** (page 198)

1. In a small saucepan, bring ¼ cup of the sugar and the water to a simmer over medium-high heat. Add the rhubarb and salt and cook, stirring, until the rhubarb has completely broken down and the mixture has slightly thickened and darkened, about 5 minutes. Transfer to a small bowl and refrigerate to cool completely.

2. In a medium bowl, whisk the crème fraîche with 1½ tablespoons of the sugar and half the vanilla seeds until the sugar has dissolved and the cream is beginning to thicken. Fold in the chilled rhubarb jam.

3. Add the strawberries to a large bowl. Sprinkle the remaining 2½ tablespoons sugar and the remaining vanilla seeds on top and gently stir to combine. Allow the berries to sit for 10 to 15 minutes, tossing occasionally, until juicy and glossy. Slice the biscuits in half, spoon the strawberries on the bottom halves, spoon the rhubarb cream on top of the strawberries, and place the other halves of the biscuits on top.

sweet
things

It's always 5 o'clock somewhere (it's not literally, that's not how time zones work!), and it's always someone's birthday, graduation, or anniversary somewhere, too. And that, my friends, is a good enough reason for a treat after any meal. We know what you grew up hearing: no dessert until you finish dinner! But here is the loophole: these aren't desserts, they are sweet things. They are snacks you can enjoy any time of the day! (We acknowledge this might be a shoddy argument, but we stand by it.)

tiramisù tres leches

gas station cherry hand pies

Where I grew up, we had gas stations that sold honest-to-goodness homemade hand pies. I never learned exactly whose home they were made in, but I did know they were delicious. Fill the hatchback, get a snick-snack! Way before I met Jesse, I said, "If I ever write a cookbook, you can bet your ass I'm putting a Gas Station Cherry Pie in it!" So fill 'er up! ~ **Julie**

1 pound **sweet cherries**, fresh or frozen, pitted (about 2½ cups)

½ cup **granulated sugar**

2½ tablespoons **cornstarch** or **tapioca flour**

3 tablespoons **fresh lemon juice**

¼ teaspoon **vanilla extract**

¼ teaspoon **kosher salt**

1 large **egg**

1 tablespoon **water**

All-purpose flour

2 chilled discs of **piecrust dough** (Go-To Piecrust, page 208)

¾ cup **turbinado sugar**

1. In a large saucepan, toss the cherries with the granulated sugar, cornstarch, 2 tablespoons of the lemon juice, the vanilla, and salt until well coated. Bring to a simmer over medium-high heat, stirring frequently. Reduce the heat to medium and simmer, stirring to prevent scorching on the bottom, until very thick, about 5 minutes. Remove the pot from the heat, stir in the remaining tablespoon lemon juice, and let the filling cool completely, stirring occasionally.

2. Preheat the oven to 400°F. Line two baking sheets with parchment paper.

3. In a small bowl, lightly beat the egg with the water and set aside.

4. On a lightly floured surface, roll out one of the discs of dough to a ⅛-inch thickness. Use a 4-inch round cookie cutter to stamp out as many circles as you can, then place on the baking sheets about 1 inch apart. Reroll the excess dough and stamp out more circles; you should get 12 to 14 circles. Scoop about 1 rounded tablespoon of the cooled filling (3 to 4 cherries and some of the syrup) into the center of each circle. With a pastry brush (or your finger), dampen about ½ inch of the edge of each circle all the way around with the egg wash. Fold the circles in half over the filling so the edges meet and gently press together. Lightly flour the tines of a fork, then lightly press around the edges of the pies to seal. Place the unbaked pies in the refrigerator while you stamp out and fill the rest. (You'll end up with some leftover cherry filling—put it on ice cream!)

5. Brush the tops of the pies with the egg wash, then generously sprinkle turbinado sugar on top of each pie. Return the pies to the baking sheets. Use a paring knife to cut 3 small slits in the top of each pie. Bake the pies for 18 to 24 minutes, rotating the pans halfway through, until golden brown and the filling is beginning to bubble through the slits. Let cool on the baking sheets for about 5 minutes, then transfer to a wire rack. Serve warm or at room temperature.

double-crust rosemary peach pie

MAKES ONE
9-INCH
DOUBLE-CRUST PIE

In L.A., rosemary grows everywhere like a sweet, fragrant, and beautiful weed. Ugh, here I go again, bragging about my rosemary. People back East think of it as a winter herb, but on the West Coast we use it in summer, when ripe peaches are plentiful (though 2 to 3 pounds of thawed frozen peach slices work in this recipe too!). The combination is surprisingly delightful. This pie takes a double crust. I recommend rolling out one disc while the other one hangs back in the fridge, then roll out the top crust after you have added the filling. ~Jesse

8 large, ripe **peaches** (about 3½ pounds; see headnote)

1 cup **granulated sugar**

¼ cup plus 2 tablespoons **all-purpose flour**, plus more as needed

Finely grated zest and juice of 1 **lemon**

2 teaspoons finely minced **fresh rosemary**

¼ teaspoon **kosher salt**

2 chilled discs of **piecrust dough** (Go-To Piecrust, page 208)

1½ tablespoons **unsalted butter**, thinly sliced

1 large **egg yolk**, beaten with 2 tablespoons water

2 to 3 tablespoons **turbinado sugar**

Vanilla ice cream or **whipped cream**

1. Bring a large pot of water to a boil and fill a large stainless-steel bowl with ice water. Using a sharp knife, make a shallow *X* in the bottom of each peach. Carefully lower the peaches into the boiling water and blanch for 2 to 3 minutes, until the skins start to loosen around the cuts. Use a slotted spoon to transfer the peaches to the ice water to cool. Drain the water, peel the peaches, then remove pits and cut into ¾-inch wedges.

2. Whisk together the granulated sugar, flour, lemon zest and juice, rosemary, and salt in a large bowl. Add the peaches and, using a rubber spatula, toss to combine.

3. Preheat the oven to 400°F. Line a baking sheet with aluminum foil.

4. Lightly flour your rolling pin. On a lightly floured surface, roll out one disc of dough, keeping the other in the fridge. Turn the round of dough slightly every few rolls, and dust the surface underneath with flour again as needed to prevent sticking. Roll until you have a 12-inch round, about ⅛ inch thick. Roll the dough around the rolling pin and transfer to a 9-inch glass pie pan. Place the pie pan in the refrigerator to chill. Roll out the other round of dough to a 12-inch round.

5. Pour the peaches and their juices into the chilled pie shell and scatter the butter on top. Place the other round of dough on top and press the edges together to seal. Trim the overhang to ½ inch, then fold the edge of the pie dough under itself and crimp as desired. Brush the top crust with the egg wash and cut a few slits in the top. Sprinkle the turbinado sugar evenly on the piecrust.

6. Place the pie pan on the baking sheet (to catch any overflowing juices) and bake for 30 minutes. Reduce the oven temperature to 375°F and continue baking until the crust is deep golden brown and the juices are bubbling, another 40 to 50 minutes. If the edges of the pie start turning too dark, cover with strips of aluminum foil.

7. Let the pie cool completely on a wire rack before slicing. Serve with vanilla ice cream or whipped cream.

tip from julie

If you are taking the time to make your pie pretty with crimps (and why wouldn't you?), your crust may become a tad warm. Don't be shy about putting your completed pie into the freezer for five or ten minutes to reset before transferring it to the oven to bake.

go-to piecrust

If piecrust was my karate, then Julie was my Mr. Miyagi. For something with so few ingredients, there are actually quite a few ways you can screw up a piecrust. I know, because I have done many of them. All I can tell you is that I was unable to make piecrust without crying until Julie taught me her method. She didn't reinvent the wheel, but she has a whole bag of tricks to make sure it all works. Now, this piecrust is like that trustworthy friend in high school whom you called upon so many times that you memorized the phone number and could dial it in the dark. (The references in this headnote are for those old enough to remember rotary phones and *The Karate Kid*.) Follow this recipe closely and you will be rewarded with perfect piecrust every time. It's simple, easy, and foolproof. ~ *Jesse*

2½ cups **all-purpose flour**

2 teaspoons **sugar**

1 teaspoon **kosher salt**

1 cup (2 sticks) **unsalted butter**, cut into ½-inch dice and chilled in the freezer for at least 20 minutes

½ cup **ice water**

1. In the bowl of a food processor, combine the flour, sugar, and salt. Pulse for about 10 seconds, until combined. Add the butter and pulse until the mixture is mealy and several pea-size pieces of butter remain, about 10 seconds.

2. Add half the ice water and pulse for 3 seconds. Add the remaining ice water and process until large clumps begin to form and no dry flour remains, 10 to 15 seconds. *Do not overmix*. You should still be able to see small flecks of butter.

3. Divide the dough evenly between two pieces of plastic wrap. Use the wrap to help gather the crumbly dough together and press into two 5-inch discs. Wrap each disc tightly in plastic wrap and chill in the refrigerator for at least 45 minutes. (The dough will keep in the refrigerator for up to 3 days or in the freezer for about 6 months.)

1. Oh, and one more tip: When you're rolling the crust out, feel free to dust the rolling pin and the top of the dough with a little flour. Turn the round of dough slightly every few rolls and re-dust the surface underneath with flour as needed to prevent sticking.

JULIE'S GOLDEN RULES

FLOUR POWER: Our go-to flour brands for piecrusts are King Arthur and Gold Medal, because of their higher protein content. We follow the spoon and level method to measure: use a spoon to scoop the flour into the measuring cup until it is mounded on top. You can gently shake the cup to let the flour settle, but do not pack the flour down. Then use the back of a butter knife or other flat edge to scrape across the top of the measuring cup. (If you are getting super-nerdy about it and using a scale, 1 cup of all-purpose flour equals about 5 ounces.)

YA GOTTA CHILL, DUDE: Cold butter and ice water are imperative in achieving a flaky crust. Not only do those components need to be frigid but so does your completed crust. Returning the dough to the refrigerator after you have pulled it together will keep the butter from melting and make the crust easier to roll out. You should always be able to see flecks of butter in the dough; they're what make the finished crust flaky. It's okay to treat your dough like a child. If the crust starts to get overheated, send it to a time-out in the refrigerator until it chills. You are the boss here!

TAKE THE TIME TO PROCESS:
The biggest aha moment for me was bringing these few simple ingredients together in a food processor. Yes, you can achieve a successful crust with a makeshift pastry cutter of two forks or knives, but why? For me, making a crust without the help of a food processor is like Cinderella getting ready for the ball without the help of her Fairy Godmother. Bibbidi, Bobbidi, Noooooo.

old-fashioned yellow cake

WITH FUDGE
FROSTING

What you've envisioned about most Southern kitchens is true: there is never a time when something isn't cooking on the stove or baking in the oven. Growing up, I was slightly intimidated by the powerhouse women who ruled our kitchen. Extra excitement was always in the air when my great-aunt, Mattie Moody, settled in because that meant the promise of her famous yellow cake with fudge frosting. For years I have pined over this cake. What was her secret? After digging through some of my mom's old recipe books, I found Mattie's recipe card tucked away in the back. The code to her yellow cake was in my hand and the mystery was finally solved: boxed cake mix and imitation butter flavoring! The spirit of that dessert and what it meant to me didn't change, though. In fact, it just moved me to create this new old-fashioned cake recipe for my kids—and maybe their kids. One that won't get lost in a family album. ~Julie

CAKE

Nonstick cooking spray

2½ cups sifted **cake flour**, plus more as needed

3 large **egg whites** and 6 **egg yolks**, room temperature

1¾ cups **granulated sugar**

10 tablespoons (1¼ sticks) **unsalted butter**, melted and cooled slightly

1 cup **buttermilk**, room temperature

¼ cup **vegetable oil**

1 tablespoon **vanilla extract**

1¼ teaspoons **baking powder**

¼ teaspoon **baking soda**

½ teaspoon **kosher salt**

FUDGE FROSTING

4 ounces **bittersweet chocolate**, finely chopped

1¼ cups (2½ sticks) **unsalted butter**, cut into dice, cool but pliable

½ cup **confectioners' sugar**, sifted

¾ cup unsweetened **cocoa powder**, sifted

½ tablespoon **instant espresso powder**, sifted

¼ teaspoon **salt**

2 teaspoons **vanilla extract**

2 to 4 tablespoons **whole milk**

1. Make the cake: Preheat the oven to 350°F. Arrange a rack in the center of the oven. Line the bottoms of two 8- or 9-inch round cake pans with parchment paper, grease the bottoms and sides with nonstick spray, and sprinkle some flour on the bottoms of each pan. Tap to shake out any excess flour. (I use 9-inch pans because I like a higher frosting-to-cake ratio, but 8-inch pans work just fine.)

2. In a medium bowl, use a handheld mixer (or a stand mixer with the whisk attachment) to whisk the egg whites until frothy and foamy, 30 to 40 seconds. Slowly add ¼ cup of the sugar and continue to whisk until the whites just begin to hold stiff peaks.

3. In another medium bowl or measuring cup, whisk together the melted butter, buttermilk, vegetable oil, vanilla, and egg yolks until thoroughly combined.

4. In a large bowl, whisk together the 2½ cups cake flour, the baking powder, baking soda, salt, and the remaining 1½ cups sugar until thoroughly combined. Add the buttermilk mixture and use a rubber spatula to stir until just incorporated. Fold in one-third

recipe continues . . .

of the egg whites until no streaks remain. Fold in the remaining egg whites until just combined.

5. Divide the batter between the cake pans. Carefully tap the cake pans on the counter a few times to release any air bubbles. Bake until a toothpick inserted in the center of the cakes comes out clean, 20 to 25 minutes. Transfer the cake pans to a wire rack and let the cakes cool in the pans for 5 minutes. Run a flexible knife around the edges of the cakes to loosen, then turn the cakes out onto a wire rack to cool completely.

6. Make the frosting: Place the chocolate in a microwave-safe bowl and heat in 30-second intervals, stirring between each interval, until melted. Let the chocolate cool.

7. Add the butter to the bowl of a stand mixer fitted with the paddle attachment and beat at medium speed until light and fluffy, 3 to 4 minutes. Add the melted chocolate and beat until creamy. Use a flexible spatula to scrape down the sides of the bowl and the paddle.

8. Whisk together the confectioners' sugar, cocoa powder, instant espresso, and salt. With the mixer running on low, gradually add this to the butter mixture. Add the vanilla and beat until well combined. Add the milk, 1 tablespoon at a time, until the frosting is spreadable but with a thick and fudgy consistency. (If making ahead, store the frosting in an airtight container or piping bag in the fridge, and let it come to room temperature before using it.)

9. Trim the top crusts from the cakes with a serrated knife (to help the cake absorb more frosting). Place one layer cut side up on a cake stand or plate. Spoon about a cup of frosting in the center and then, using an offset spatula or the back of a spoon, spread it around into an even layer. Place the second cake, cut side down, on top of the frosted layer. Frost the top and sides of the cake with the remaining frosting. If not serving it immediately, cover the cake with a dome or large bowl. The cake will keep for up to 24 hours at room temperature.

This is Jesse popping in for a moment. I have to give you the tiniest bit of back story on this frosting. Julie probably made fourteen versions of it before landing on this one. Every variation was delicious, but she became obsessed with which one best suited the buttery cake. There were tears, there was laughter, there was me begging her to pick one version. I am so proud of the frosting we landed on, but if you want a different one, keep an eye out for Julie's next book: *13 Fudge Frostings and the Reason My Husband Will Never Eat Cake Again.* ～ Jesse

tiramisù
tres
leches

I would like to start a support group for those of us with partners who don't enjoy sweets. My husband, Justin, is not a dessert person. It's been tough on me, and I grapple with this every day, but I'm learning to live with it. One year, for his birthday, his co-workers knew better than to get him a cake and opted instead for a pile of french fries, complete with candles. Personally, I would cry if anyone tried to pull that move on me, but for Justin it was perfect.

The one dessert he can't refuse, though, is tiramisù. He even asks for it at restaurants that would never in a million years offer it: "Mmmm, that hamachi sushi was delicious. I wonder if they have tiramisù here?" So, obviously we had to present our own version for this book. This long-established classic is given a new spin here. Gone are the traditional ladyfingers and in their place is a delicious tres leches cake, inspired by the milk-soaked Mexican classic. Try it for yourself and see why this dessert is "Justin approved."

The cake does need at least four hours to set, so make sure you plan ahead! ~ Jesse

CAKE
Nonstick cooking spray

¾ cup (1½ sticks) **unsalted butter**, room temperature

1½ cups **sugar**

6 large **eggs**

1 teaspoon **vanilla extract**

2¼ cups **all-purpose flour**

1½ teaspoons **baking powder**

1 teaspoon **kosher salt**

¾ teaspoon **ground cinnamon**

BOOZY CAFFEINATED MILK SOAK
½ cup **whole milk**

½ cup strong **brewed coffee**, room temperature

1 (14-ounce) can **sweetened condensed milk**

1 (12-ounce) can **evaporated milk**

1 tablespoon **instant espresso powder**

3 tablespoons **rum** or **cognac**

MASCARPONE CREAM
8 large **egg yolks**

1 cup **sugar**

1½ cups **heavy cream**

2 cups (16 ounces) **mascarpone cheese**

ASSEMBLY
Cocoa powder or **chocolate shavings**

1. Make the cake: Preheat the oven to 350°F. Lightly coat a 9 by 13-inch baking dish with nonstick cooking spray.

2. In the bowl of a stand mixer fitted with the paddle attachment, cream the butter and sugar until light and fluffy, 4 to 5 minutes. Add the eggs, one at a time, and mix until thoroughly combined. Add the vanilla and mix to incorporate.

3. In a medium bowl, whisk together the flour, baking powder, salt, and cinnamon. With the mixer running on low speed, add the flour mixture to the creamed butter in two additions and beat until just combined, scraping down the sides of the bowl if needed.

4. Pour the batter into the baking dish. Bake until a toothpick inserted into the center comes out clean, 28 to 30 minutes. Let cool completely.

recipe continues . . .

5. **Make the milk soak:** In a large liquid measuring cup with a spout, whisk together the milk, coffee, condensed milk, evaporated milk, espresso powder, and rum until smooth.

6. Poke the cake all over with a wooden skewer. Gradually pour the milk mixture all over the cake, letting it soak in through the holes. If any liquid pools on the surface of the cake or along the sides, just spoon it back over the cake until it is absorbed. It may take 15 minutes for all of the milk to soak in.

7. **Make the cream:** Fill a medium pot with 1 inch of water and bring to a simmer.

Set a double boiler or medium heatproof bowl on top. Add the egg yolks and ½ cup of the sugar and cook, whisking constantly, until the yolks lighten and thicken, the sugar dissolves completely, and the mixture reaches 165°F, about 7 minutes.

8. Transfer the egg mixture to the bowl of a stand mixer fitted with the whisk attachment and whip on medium speed until very pale yellow and thick and the bowl is cool to the touch, about 5 minutes. Transfer the mixture to a large bowl.

9. Wipe out the stand mixer bowl and add the cream and remaining ½ cup sugar.

Whip on medium speed until medium-soft peaks form, about 4 minutes. Add the mascarpone and continue to whip until soft and spreadable with medium peaks, about 2 minutes more. Fold the mascarpone mixture into the egg yolk mixture until smooth.

10. **Assemble the cake:** Spread the cream evenly over the cake. Chill the cake in the refrigerator for at least 4 hours, but ideally for 24 hours. Before serving, dust a little cocoa powder on the top or sprinkle with chocolate shavings.

fudge brownies

Listen, if I am going to be given the choice between cake or brownies, I am going to go with cake. Jesse, however, *loves* brownies, so I indulged him and created this fudgy treat that is rich enough to make my body tingle. (Please let it be the cayenne pepper and not early-onset menopause.) Like a hot flash, these slightly spicy brownies take you on a journey! If you're making them for kids, just leave out the cayenne. It will be more King Triton's Carousel than Mr. Toad's Wild Ride. ~ Julie

SPICY PEANUT BUTTER SWIRL

3 tablespoons **unsalted butter**, melted

½ cup **crunchy peanut butter** (a regular old supermarket brand, not the natural stuff)

¼ cup **confectioners' sugar**

½ teaspoon **ground cinnamon**

½ teaspoon **cayenne pepper**

¼ teaspoon **kosher salt**

BROWNIES

Nonstick cooking spray

10 tablespoons (1¼ sticks) **unsalted butter**

5 ounces **70–72% dark chocolate**, finely chopped

1¼ cups **granulated sugar**

2 tablespoons **unsweetened cocoa powder**

½ teaspoon **kosher salt**

1 teaspoon **vanilla extract**

3 large **eggs**, room temperature

1 cup **all-purpose flour**

1. **Make the peanut butter swirl:** In a medium bowl, whisk together the melted butter, peanut butter, confectioners' sugar, cinnamon, cayenne, and salt until smooth.

2. **Make the brownies:** Preheat the oven to 350°F. Line a 9-inch square cake pan or baking dish with parchment paper, leaving a 1-inch overhang. Coat with nonstick cooking spray.

3. Combine the butter and chocolate in a large, heatproof bowl. Melt in the microwave until smooth, stirring every 30 seconds, about 1 minute total. Add the sugar, cocoa powder, salt, and vanilla and whisk until smooth. Add the eggs, one at a time, whisking well after each addition. Use a rubber spatula to fold in the flour. Do not overmix.

4. Transfer the batter to the baking dish. Dollop the peanut butter mixture on top of the brownie batter and use a butter knife to swirl it through. Bake until a toothpick inserted in the center comes out almost clean, but with a few moist crumbs attached, 25 to 30 minutes. Let cool completely in the pan before cutting into 16 brownies.

biscochito cookie bars

I didn't even know this was a thing, but apparently in 1989 the biscochito became the official cookie of the state of New Mexico. As someone who is obsessed with cookies, I am disappointed that I missed this landmark occasion. I was fourteen, and what else was I doing with my time? I should have known about this!

Well, I am thrilled to right my wrong by offering a fresh spin on this New Mexican holiday cookie classic. I love the subtle licorice flavor that the anise brings to these sweet-salty-buttery blondie/ shortbread-like cookies. The classic version of this recipe calls for lard. I know, *lard!* Using butter instead makes for the chewiest cookie bars with crunchy golden edges. A finishing pinch of flaky salt, and you have the perfectly balanced treat. Even the most traditional sweets deserve a makeover! ~ Jesse

- 11 tablespoons **unsalted butter**, room temperature, plus more as needed
- 2 cups **all-purpose flour**
- 1 teaspoon **baking powder**
- ¾ teaspoon **kosher salt**
- 1 teaspoon **anise seeds**, plus more for topping
- 1 teaspoon **ground cinnamon**
- ¾ cup **granulated sugar**
- ¾ cup firmly packed **light brown sugar**
- 1 large **egg**, room temperature
- 2 teaspoons **anise extract**
- 1 teaspoon **vanilla extract**
- **Flaky sea salt**

1. Preheat the oven to 350°F. Grease a 9-inch square baking dish with a little butter, then line with parchment paper, leaving a 2-inch overhang (this will make it easy to lift the bars from the pan).

2. In a medium bowl, whisk together the flour, baking powder, salt, anise seeds, and cinnamon.

3. In the bowl of a stand mixer fitted with the paddle attachment, beat the 11 tablespoons butter and the sugars on medium speed until creamy and fluffy, 3 to 4 minutes. Scrape down the sides of the bowl, then add the egg, anise extract, and vanilla. Beat until fluffy, scraping down the bowl once or twice, another 3 minutes. Gradually add the flour mixture to the butter mixture, beating on low speed until just combined. The dough will be crumbly.

4. Scrape the dough into the baking dish and use a rubber spatula to press it down in an even layer. Sprinkle more anise seeds and some flaky sea salt evenly over the dough. Bake until golden around the edges and a toothpick inserted in the center comes out clean, about 25 minutes. Let cool in the pan for 15 minutes. Use the parchment as a sling to lift the cake from the pan and place on a wire rack to cool completely, then slice into 16 bars.

not your church lady's strawberry semifreddo

Semifreddo means "semi-frozen," and on the dessert spectrum it's positioned right in that sweet spot between frozen mousse and ice cream. It's also what I like to call myself after an afternoon of skiing: "Mama is semifreddo, so start a fire!" This dessert was conceived out of my love of strawberry pretzel salad. I acknowledge that "strawberry pretzel salad" sounds like I just threw three nouns together, but I promise you, it's an actual thing in the South. I'm pretty sure it was born from that crazy "make it in a Jell-O mold and call it a salad" craze of the '50s.

We have freed this Middle American classic from the unnecessary burden of being in the salad family, and it now lives loud and proud as a layered, creamy, fruity dessert with a salty crunch. This does need at least six hours in the freezer, so don't try to whip it up right before dinner! ~ **Julie**

PRETZEL CRUNCH

- 2½ cups (about 3½ ounces) salted **mini pretzels**
- 3 tablespoons **nonfat milk powder**
- ¼ cup packed **light brown sugar**
- 2 tablespoons **granulated sugar**
- ½ teaspoon **kosher salt**
- 10 tablespoons (1¼ sticks) **unsalted butter**, melted

SEMIFREDDO

- 1½ pounds **fresh strawberries**, hulled and quartered (about 4½ cups)
- ½ cup plus 3 tablespoons **granulated sugar**
- 1 tablespoon plus 2 teaspoons **fresh lemon juice**
- 8 ounces **cream cheese**, softened
- ⅔ cup **sweetened condensed milk**
- ¼ teaspoon **kosher salt**
- 1½ cups **heavy cream**

1. **Make the pretzel crunch:** Preheat the oven to 275°F. Line a baking sheet with parchment paper. Line a 9 by 5-inch loaf pan crosswise with parchment paper so that there is at least 1 inch of overhang on each side.

2. In a medium bowl, crumble the pretzels with your hands, breaking them up into ¼- to ½-inch pieces. Add the milk powder, sugars, and salt and toss to combine. Pour in 7 tablespoons of the melted butter and toss until the pretzels are well coated.

3. Spread the pretzel mixture on the baking sheet. Bake, stirring once halfway through, until the pretzels are lightly toasted, 20 to 25 minutes. Let cool completely.

4. Set aside ½ cup of the pretzel crunch for topping, then transfer the remainder to a food processor. Add the remaining 3 tablespoons melted butter. Pulse for five 1-second bursts. Scrape down the sides of the bowl, then pulse about 5 more times, until the pretzels are broken down into small crumbs, but are not completely uniform or pulverized. Press the mixture in an even layer into the loaf pan. Freeze until ready to use.

recipe continues . . .

5. Make the semifreddo: In a medium pot over medium heat, combine the strawberries and ½ cup sugar. Cook, stirring occasionally, until the strawberries have broken down into a thick, chunky jam and have reduced to about 1 cup, 15 to 20 minutes. Remove the pot from the heat and stir in 1 tablespoon of the lemon juice. Let the strawberry jam cool completely.

6. In the bowl of a stand mixer fitted with the whisk attachment, combine the cream cheese, condensed milk, salt, and remaining 2 teaspoons lemon juice. Mix on medium speed for 1 minute. Scrape down the sides of the bowl, then continue mixing on medium-high speed until totally smooth and slightly fluffy, about 1 minute more. Transfer to a medium bowl.

7. In the stand mixer bowl (no need to clean it), combine the cream and remaining 3 tablespoons sugar. Whip on medium-high speed until the cream holds medium-stiff peaks, 2 to 3 minutes.

8. Add a large scoop of the whipped cream to the bowl with the cream cheese mixture and gently stir together. Pour the cream cheese mixture into the bowl with the whipped cream and fold together just until no streaks remain. Gently fold in half the strawberry jam, just enough to create streaks, then gently fold in the remaining jam. The mixture should look marbled, with pockets of jam. Transfer the semifreddo mixture to the loaf pan with the pretzel crust and freeze until firm, at least 6 hours and up to 3 days.

9. When ready to serve, use the parchment paper to lift the semifreddo out of the pan and place on a flat surface. Let sit at room temperature for about 15 minutes, then sprinkle with the reserved pretzel crunch, slice, and serve.

---

note

To store leftover semifreddo (if you have any!), use the parchment paper to transfer the loaf back to the loaf pan and cover with plastic wrap. Leftovers will keep in the freezer for up to 1 week. The crunch can also be made ahead and will keep in an airtight container at room temperature for 1 week or in the fridge or freezer for 1 month.

banana cream pavlova

As Gwen Stefani once stated so beautifully, "This sh*t is bananas. B-A-N-A-N-A-S!" Bow down, because the Holy Trinity is in our presence: banana cream, banana liqueur, and vanilla wafers piled atop meringue that's baked crunchy on the outside and chewy on the inside.

The stacked combination of fruit, creamy things, and meringue is named a pavlova, after the Russian ballerina Anna "The Banana" Pavlova. We don't have proof that this was her nickname, but we also don't have proof that it wasn't her nickname. After one bite of this decadent dessert you'll be doing a grand jeté into a dying swan, just as Anna Pavlova did in 1905. (Look it up on YouTube!) ~ Julie

MERINGUE
Nonstick cooking spray
¼ cup **cornstarch**
1 tablespoon **distilled white vinegar**
1 tablespoon **vanilla extract**
2 cups **superfine sugar**
8 large **egg whites**, room temperature (see Note, page 225)
1½ teaspoons **kosher salt**

BANANA CREAM
2 cups (16 ounces) **mascarpone cheese**
½ cup sifted **confectioners' sugar**
1 tablespoon **vanilla extract**
½ teaspoon **kosher salt**
1¾ cups **heavy cream**
3 medium **bananas**, peeled and sliced into ¼-inch rounds

ASSEMBLY
¼ cup **heavy cream**
¼ cup **banana liqueur**
45 **vanilla wafer cookies**, 30 left whole and 15 crushed

1. Make the meringue: Preheat the oven to 250°F. Line two baking sheets with parchment paper.

2. Place a 9-inch round cake pan in the center of one of the pieces of parchment paper and use a pencil to trace a circle around the outside of the pan. Flip the sheet of parchment paper over so the marked side is face down. Repeat with the remaining sheet of parchment. Coat the parchment with nonstick spray.

3. In a small bowl, stir together the cornstarch, vinegar, and vanilla. In the bowl of a stand mixer fitted with the whisk attachment, beat the superfine sugar, egg whites, and salt on low speed until combined. Increase the speed to medium high and beat until soft peaks form, about 7 minutes. Add the cornstarch mixture to the egg whites and continue beating until medium peaks form and the mixture is glossy, about 5 more minutes.

4. Divide the meringue between the prepared baking sheets, spooning into the traced circles. Use the back of a spoon to spread the meringues to fill the 9-inch circles, creating a shallow well in the center and a 1-inch lip around the sides. Transfer the meringues to the oven and bake for 90 minutes, until firm to the touch. Turn off the oven, open the oven door slightly (prop open with a wooden spoon, if needed), and let the meringues cool gradually, 1 to 2 hours.

recipe continues . . .

5. **Make the banana cream:** In the bowl of a stand mixer fitted with the whisk attachment, combine the mascarpone, confectioners' sugar, vanilla, and salt. Mix on medium-low speed until well combined, about 30 seconds. With the mixer running on low speed, slowly drizzle in the cream. Once the cream is incorporated, increase the mixer speed to medium and mix until soft peaks form, 2 to 3 minutes. Add the banana slices and gently fold in with a rubber spatula.

6. **Assemble the pavlova:** Gently peel the parchment paper from one of the meringues, and using a large spatula, transfer the layer to a cake stand or serving platter. Spoon about one-third of the banana cream into the well of the meringue and spread evenly.

7. In a pie pan or shallow bowl, stir together the cream and liqueur. Working in batches, place the whole vanilla wafers in a single layer in the cream-liqueur mixture and let soak for 20 seconds, then flip and soak for another 20 seconds on the other side. Arrange the soaked cookies in a single layer over the banana cream. Spoon another one-third of the banana cream over the cookies and gently spread in an even layer. Place the second meringue layer on top and spread with the remaining banana cream. Let sit for about 10 minutes.

8. Sprinkle the pavlova with the crushed vanilla wafers. Slice the pavlova with a serrated knife, then serve immediately.

egg-cellent tips

What do you mean I can't take a yolk? Actually, you can! May we suggest saving the egg yolks leftover here for the Coconut Pudding on page 226? Here's another egg-cellent tip: You can freeze egg whites until you are ready to use them. So, when you are making those recipes that call for only yolks, save the whites for a future endeavor!

coconut pudding

It's not easy to convince kids that Mom's version is better than the store-bought stuff. Just like my handmade Halloween costumes are always cuter than the ones I can order online, my homemade coconut pudding is way more exciting than the packaged kind that my kids always crave. With the sweet and salty cornflake crunch topping, it didn't take much convincing to win them over. American-style pudding is one of my favorite desserts because you can do so many things with it. Not only is it delicious just as it is, but it can also be piped into cupcakes, used as pie filling, or spread between cake layers. Okay, I'm off to start sewing Josephine's and Henry's Halloween costumes. They are going as Coconut Pudding and Coconut-Cornflake Crunch. ~ Julie

PUDDING

1 cup **granulated sugar**

¼ cup **cornstarch**

½ teaspoon **kosher salt**

8 large **egg yolks**

2 (14-ounce) cans **unsweetened full-fat coconut milk**, shaken well

1 tablespoon **coconut extract**

2 tablespoons **unsalted butter**, cut into dice, room temperature

COCONUT-CORNFLAKE CRUNCH

Nonstick cooking spray

2 cups **corn flakes**

1 cup **unsweetened coconut flakes**

¾ cup **light brown sugar**

¼ cup **light corn syrup**

6 tablespoons **unsalted butter**

¼ teaspoon **kosher salt**

1 teaspoon **vanilla extract**

½ teaspoon **baking soda**

Flaky sea salt

1. Make the pudding: In a medium saucepan, whisk together the sugar, cornstarch, and salt. Add the egg yolks and coconut milk and whisk to combine. Turn the heat to medium low and cook, whisking gently, until steaming hot, about 5 minutes. Increase the heat to medium and continue cooking until thick, about 5 minutes more. Once the custard begins to bubble, continue whisking for 2 minutes. Remove the pot from the heat and stir in the coconut extract and butter. Pour the pudding into a shallow baking dish; an 8- or 9-inch pie plate works perfectly. Cover with plastic wrap, pressing the wrap directly against the pudding to prevent a skin from forming, and let cool to room temperature, about 1 hour. Transfer to the refrigerator and chill for at least 2 hours.

2. Make the crunch: Preheat the oven to 325°F. Line a baking sheet with aluminum foil and coat lightly with nonstick cooking spray.

3. Spread the corn flakes and coconut flakes on the baking sheet in an even layer. Toast, stirring halfway through, until light golden and fragrant, 7 to 8 minutes. Transfer the baking sheet to a wire rack to cool. Reduce the oven temperature to 225°F.

4. In a large skillet, stir together the brown sugar, corn syrup, butter, and salt over medium-high heat until the butter melts and the mixture begins to bubble. Cook, stirring constantly, for 4 to 5 minutes more; the mixture will thicken and darken to a light peanut butter color. Remove the skillet from the heat and immediately stir in the vanilla and baking soda. Add the toasted corn flakes and coconut and quickly fold until well coated.

5. Grease the baking sheet again, generously, then spread the mixture in an even layer. Bake, stirring once or twice, until deep caramel in color, 20 to 25 minutes. Sprinkle

some flaky sea salt evenly over the top. Let the crunch cool on the baking sheet, then break into bite-size clusters. (Store in an airtight container at room temperature for up to 5 days.)

6. To serve, spoon the pudding into cups or bowls and top with the coconut-cornflake crunch.

Jesse here for a moment: When I was young and vacationing in the UK for the first time, I couldn't believe how obsessed the British were about pudding. "Mmmmm! The bangers and mash were delicious. Shall we be naughty and have a bit of pudding?" Every meal they talked about pudding! It was finally brought to my attention that "pudding" meant "dessert." What Americans call "pudding" they call "custard." The Brits also call bathing suits "swimming costumes" and paper towels "kitchen roll." Listen, whatever you call it, this quick (American) pudding is the perfect end to any meal. ~*Jesse*

butter pecan caramels

MAKES ABOUT 50, DEPENDING ON HOW YOU CUT THEM

Sometimes when I am considering what flavors I want in a dessert, I think about my favorite kinds of ice cream. I mean, as far as dessert flavor combinations are concerned, ice cream innovators are pretty much the masters in the field. My favorite has always been butter pecan, so when we created this caramel, that's the combination that went right to the top of the list. Runners-up were Gooey Butter Cake and Pistachio and Honey. (Here's a shout-out to our favorite mad ice cream scientist, Jeni Britton Bauer, who founded @jenisicecreams!)

Okay, back to caramels. I love making these and individually wrapping them as holiday host gifts. There's just something so thoughtful about giving homemade candy—and these will make your host have second thoughts about everyone who brought bottles of schnapps or scented candles. And really, isn't gift-giving what the holidays are all about?

~Jesse

Nonstick cooking spray

1 cup chopped raw **pecans**

7 tablespoons **unsalted butter**

1 cup **heavy cream**

¼ cup **honey**

¼ cup **light corn syrup**

¾ cup **light brown sugar**

½ **vanilla bean**, seeds scraped, or ½ teaspoon **vanilla bean paste**

½ teaspoon **kosher salt**

1½ tablespoons **bourbon**

Flaky sea salt, for topping

1. Line an 8-inch square baking dish with 2 overlapping sheets of parchment paper so there is overhang on all sides. Coat the parchment paper with nonstick cooking spray.

2. Add the pecans to a small dry skillet and toast over medium heat, stirring occasionally, until toasty and fragrant, about 5 minutes.

3. In a medium saucepan fitted with a candy thermometer, melt the butter over medium-low heat, swirling and tilting the pan to coat a few inches up the sides. In a medium bowl, whisk together the cream, honey, corn syrup, brown sugar, vanilla seeds, and salt until smooth. Pour the mixture into the melted butter and whisk to incorporate, being careful to avoid sloshing the mixture up the sides. Increase the heat to medium and bring to a boil. Cook, without stirring, until the mixture reaches 250° to 255°F (between soft ball and hard ball stages), anywhere between 10 and 20 minutes, depending on your stovetop. Do not let the mixture exceed 255°F, or it will become too hard and brittle.

4. Remove the pan from the heat and work quickly to carefully pour in the bourbon; the mixture will bubble dramatically. Add the pecans and stir briefly to coat. Pour the pecan mixture into the baking dish. Let sit at room temperature until firm, 2 to 4 hours.

5. Use the parchment paper to lift the caramel from the pan. Cut into 1-inch squares. (To store, keep in an airtight container in layers separated by wax or parchment paper, or wrap individually in small wax paper squares. The caramels will keep at room temperature for up to 2 weeks.)

freezer mint cookies

Is it cruelty or a godsend that every year, right after the holiday season, those adolescent cookie peddlers start knockin' on our doors and setting up their stands outside of every supermarket? If you are like me, you break down early and buy as many Thin Mints as you can without looking like a hoarder and then you quarantine them in the back of the freezer to be rationed out for as long as possible. No matter how much restraint I exercise, they never last as long as I need them to. The timing never ceases to amaze me; just as I am finishing the last sleeve of those frozen cookies, the girls in green disappear, not to be seen again until next winter. Hence, this cookie. If you can believe it, these chocolate-shelled, shortbread-like mint cookies are almost more addictive than the originals that inspired them. I love them so much I am thinking about selling them door to door between the months of April and December. ~ **Julie**

COOKIES

- ½ cup **all-purpose flour**
- ¾ cup **whole wheat flour**
- ½ teaspoon **kosher salt**
- ½ cup **Dutch-process cocoa powder**
- 1 cup **confectioners' sugar**, sifted
- 1 teaspoon **baking powder**
- ¾ cup (1½ sticks) **unsalted butter**, cut into dice and chilled in freezer for at least 20 minutes
- 1 tablespoon **molasses**
- 1 teaspoon **peppermint extract**

CHOCOLATE SHELL

- 8 ounces **milk chocolate**, chopped
- 8 ounces **70% or higher dark chocolate**, chopped
- ⅓ cup **refined coconut oil**
- ⅛ teaspoon **kosher salt**
- 1 teaspoon **peppermint extract**

1. Make the cookies: Add the flours, salt, cocoa powder, confectioners' sugar, and baking powder to the bowl of a food processor and pulse until well combined, about 1 minute. Add the butter, molasses, and peppermint extract and pulse until the butter is incorporated and the dough just comes together, about 1 minute more.

2. Turn the dough out onto a sheet of parchment paper and press into a disc. Cover with another sheet of parchment and transfer to the refrigerator to chill for about 15 minutes.

3. Preheat the oven to 350°F. Line two baking sheets with parchment paper.

4. Roll out the chilled dough to a ¼-inch thickness. Using a 2-inch round cutter, stamp out cookies and place them on the baking sheets, spacing about 1 inch apart. Reroll the scraps up to two times as needed and stamp out more cookies. Bake for 15 to 18 minutes, rotating the pans halfway, until the tops are dry looking. Let cool on the baking sheets for a few minutes, then transfer to a wire rack to cool completely.

5. Make the chocolate shell: Line a baking sheet with parchment or wax paper.

6. Add the milk and dark chocolates, coconut oil, and salt to a heatproof medium bowl. Microwave for 30 seconds, stir, then continue microwaving in 15-second

increments, stirring between, until melted and smooth. Stir in the peppermint extract, then let cool for about 15 minutes.

7. Arrange the cookies on the baking sheet and transfer to the freezer to chill, 15 to 20 minutes.

8. Using a fork, dip a cold cookie into the melted chocolate mixture. Turn to coat, then lift out and hold over the bowl to allow the excess to drip off. Place the coated cookie on the baking sheet and repeat with the remaining cookies (see Note). Place the baking sheet in the freezer to let the shell fully harden, about 30 minutes. (Cookies can be transferred to an airtight container and stored in the freezer for a midnight snack.)

note

Leftover chocolate shell can be kept in the fridge and melted for future use. Pour it on a scoop of ice cream and watch it harden like magic!

starters, drinks & dranks

We are born entertainers at heart. One of us even gets paid to be one. When it comes to entertaining for a dinner party, though, we both thrive. Here are some of our favorite treats to start the fun off right. And aren't we clever—putting starters at the *end* of our book? We think so; we're pleased as punch.

And, oh yeah, that reminds us; we put a few drinks in here for you, too. They're nonalcoholic, but don't worry, we have you covered: all these drinks can be converted effortlessly into cocktails if you need to make them dranks.

pimento cheese & green chile roll-ups

In the Ferguson household, these green chile rolls were a staple during the holiday season. My mom would make platters of the savory rolled-up finger treats. (Yes, finger treats. If I had called them canapés, the jig would have been up and my parents would have known I was gay. So: finger treats.) They were so addicting that one year I broke into the garage fridge, where my mom was storing them for a party, and I ate a bunch right there, on the cold cement floor, and rearranged the remaining pinwheels on the platter to cover my tracks. And you know what? I got away with it. It was thrilling. Only a career in musical theater saved me from becoming a hardened criminal. You can take away three things from this story: (1) these roll-ups are delicious; (2) musical theater saves lives; and (3) these are great make-ahead party snacks.

When Julie and I were talking about food we simply *had* to have in this book, these cheesy and spicy snacks were on the top of my list. The original recipe called for cream cheese, onion powder, and Hatch green chiles, but Julie had the brilliant idea of making our version with pimento cheese.

P.S. Yes, in my older years I am aware that my obsession with musicals is much more of a giveaway than my calling these canapés. ~*Jesse*

PIMENTO CHEESE

4 ounces extra-sharp yellow **cheddar cheese**

2 ounces **Parmesan cheese**

2 (2-ounce) jars **pimentos**, drained

½ teaspoon **dry mustard**

¼ teaspoon **garlic powder**

¼ teaspoon **cayenne pepper**

Freshly ground black **pepper** to taste

¼ cup **cream cheese**, room temperature

1 tablespoon **mayonnaise**

ASSEMBLY

6 (8-inch) **flour tortillas**

2 (4-ounce) cans diced **Hatch green chiles**, drained

1. **Make the pimento cheese:** Grate the cheeses on the large holes on a box grater. Transfer to a medium bowl. Add the pimentos, mustard, garlic powder, cayenne, pepper, cream cheese, and mayonnaise and mix until creamy and thoroughly combined.

2. **Assemble the pinwheels:** Spread 3 to 4 tablespoons of the pimento cheese over a flour tortilla. Sprinkle 2 tablespoons of diced green chiles on top. Roll the tortilla up, seal with a toothpick, and place on a plate. Repeat with the remaining ingredients. Cover the plate with plastic wrap and place in the fridge until the rolls are cold and firm, about 2 hours. (If you're in a hurry, pop in the freezer for about 10 minutes.).

3. When ready to serve, remove the toothpicks, slice each roll into ½-inch rounds, and arrange on a platter. Serve chilled or at room temperature and watch people lose their minds!

albuquerque hush puppies

More green chiles! This is something that can't be helped; I am done apologizing for it! I always keep a stockpile of canned green chiles in my pantry, and if I am lucky enough to find fresh Hatch chiles at my local grocery, I buy as many as I can, roast them in my oven or on my grill, and freeze them for later use (see Note, page 91). Green chiles are one of the ingredients that epitomize the food I was raised on. In my hometown of Albuquerque, almost every restaurant somehow offers them as an option in every dish. So, in honor of the Que (that's what locals call Albuquerque, for short), we are offering these crisp cornmeal fritters with green chile. You can certainly make them without the chiles, but then you can't call them Albuquerque Hush Puppies. They are just hush puppies at that point. ~Jesse

Grapeseed or canola oil

1 cup medium- or coarse-ground yellow cornmeal

½ cup all-purpose flour

1½ teaspoons baking powder

1 teaspoon kosher salt

¼ teaspoon freshly ground black pepper

1 teaspoon sugar

½ teaspoon garlic powder

1 large egg

1 cup buttermilk

½ medium onion, grated (on the large holes of box grater)

½ cup fresh Hatch green chiles, stemmed, seeded, and finely chopped, or 1 (4-ounce) can diced Hatch green chiles, drained

4 tablespoons (½ stick) unsalted butter, cut into ¼-inch dice and chilled in the freezer for at least 20 minutes

Crystal Hot Honey (page 47) or other honey of choice (optional)

1. Line a baking sheet or plate with paper towels. Pour 3 inches of the oil into a large, heavy-bottomed pot, making sure you have a couple inches of clearance. Heat the oil over medium heat until it reaches 350°F on a deep-fry thermometer.

2. In a large bowl, whisk together the cornmeal, flour, baking powder, salt, pepper, sugar, and garlic powder. In another medium bowl, whisk together the egg, buttermilk, onion, and chiles. Pour the wet ingredients into the dry ingredients and mix until just combined. Fold in the butter.

3. Use a spring-release ice cream scoop to gently drop about 2 tablespoons of batter into the hot oil. Repeat a couple of times to fry 4 or 5 hush puppies at a time (keep the remaining batter in the freezer while you fry), flipping once, until golden brown all over, 3 to 4 minutes. Transfer the hush puppies to the baking sheet to drain and continue to make the remaining hush puppies. Serve with honey, if desired.

broiled oysters

My Aunt Paula was vivacious, beautiful, and hilarious, as well as the fastest oyster shucker I ever knew. (She not only taught me the art of shucking but also the importance of bright red lipstick and how to put it on without using a mirror.)

Most seafood markets have shucked fresh oysters. If you don't see any, just ask your butcher or fishmonger to do the deed and save the oyster shells for you so you can broil those babies right in them. With buttery, toasty oyster cracker bread crumbs, these are a cross between fried oysters and oysters Rockefeller. I think my Aunt Paula would be proud; if she were alive today, she'd ask me, "Did you shuck 'em yourself? Good girl." ~ Julie

- ¾ cup **olive oil**
- 1 small **shallot**, finely chopped
- 1½ teaspoons **red pepper flakes**
- 1 **scallion**, white and light green parts only, finely chopped
- 1 tablespoon **unsalted butter**
- 1 cup **oyster crackers**, finely crushed
- ⅓ cup freshly grated **Parmesan cheese**
- **Kosher salt** and **freshly ground black pepper**
- 1 teaspoon finely grated **lemon zest**
- 1 tablespoon **fresh lemon juice**
- 2 tablespoons finely chopped **fresh parsley**
- 24 fresh **oysters**, rinsed
- **Rock salt** (if using oyster shells)
- **Crusty French bread**

1. In a small saucepan, combine the olive oil, shallot, red pepper flakes, and scallion. Cook over medium heat, stirring occasionally, until the shallot is golden brown and toasty, about 15 minutes. Strain through a fine-mesh sieve. Reserve ¼ cup of the oil in a medium bowl and save the rest for another use (such as in a vinaigrette).

2. In a medium skillet, melt the butter over medium heat until beginning to bubble. Add the cracker crumbs and stir to evenly coat. Cook until the crumbs are golden and toasty, about 5 minutes. Remove the pan from the heat and let the crumbs cool slightly, then stir in the fried shallot mixture and the Parmesan cheese. Season with salt and pepper.

3. Arrange an oven rack 6 inches below the broiler and preheat the broiler. If using the oyster shells, spread enough rock salt on a baking sheet to be about 1 inch thick.

4. Add the lemon zest and juice and the parsley to the bowl with the shallot oil. Gently shuck the oysters, releasing them from their shells into the bowl, and toss to coat in the oil. Return each oyster to a half shell and nestle into the bed of rock salt. Top each oyster with a spoonful of the crumb mixture. (Alternatively, if simply using shucked oysters spread the oysters in an even layer in a shallow medium baking dish and sprinkle with the crumb mixture.)

5. Broil the oysters, keeping a close eye on them so they don't burn, until the crumbs are a shade darker and the oysters are just warmed through but not really cooked, about 2 minutes. Serve immediately, with crusty French bread.

Roasted Red Pepper Dip and Smoked Trout Dip

smoked trout dip

I used to make French onion dip with sour cream and a package of dried French onion soup mix. It made me very popular; it also gave me bad breath, which made me less popular. Here's a riff on that same idea that combines everything you love about a good dip with everything you love about a Sunday-morning bagel. ~Julie

2 tablespoons minced **shallots**

Juice of ½ **lemon**

2 fillets (8 ounces total) **smoked trout**, skin removed

6 ounces **cream cheese**

⅓ cup **sour cream**

3 tablespoons finely chopped **fresh chives**

1 tablespoon finely chopped **fresh parsley**

½ teaspoon **kosher salt**

Pinch of **ground white** or **black pepper**

¼ teaspoon **paprika**

Red pepper flakes (optional)

Crackers, pita chips, or **Potato-Parsnip Hash-kes** (page 42)

1. In a small bowl, combine the shallots and lemon juice.

2. In a medium bowl, use a fork to break up the fish fillets. Stir in the cream cheese, sour cream, chives, parsley, salt, pepper, paprika, and a pinch of red pepper flakes, if using, until smooth and creamy. Stir in the shallots and lemon juice. Cover the bowl with plastic wrap and chill in the refrigerator for at least 1 hour.

3. Serve the dip chilled with crackers or pita chips, or on top of hash-kes.

roasted red pepper dip

Okay, so this dip actually was born of my frequent heartburn. I know red peppers are a heartburn trigger, but let me finish! Julie and I were tasked to create a sponsored post for an antacid I use that rhymes with the word Pepcid. Oh, well, it's actually Pepcid. We were so thrilled with this dip that we felt we should include it here. Now you, too, can #SeizeTheMeal! (that was the hashtag I had to use). This dip is inspired by a red pepper and walnut dip from the Middle East called *muhammara*. We have taken all the things we love about the original—its big flavor and subtly sweet smokiness—and have added warming spices like ginger, coriander, and turmeric. The jalapeño offers a kick of heat, while the tangy pomegranate molasses brings it back to its roots.

~Jesse

1 **whole wheat pita** (about 2 ounces), torn into bite-size pieces

1 (16-ounce) jar **roasted red peppers**, drained

1½ cups chopped **walnuts** (about 6 ounces), toasted

4 **scallions**, white and green parts, roughly chopped

1 small fresh **red chile** or **jalapeño**, stemmed, seeded, and roughly chopped

3 **garlic cloves**, smashed

3 tablespoons **olive oil**, plus more as needed

1 teaspoon finely grated **lemon zest**

Juice of 1 **lemon**

1 tablespoon **pomegranate molasses**, plus more as needed (see Note, page 102)

1 teaspoon **kosher salt**, plus more as needed

1 teaspoon **ground cumin**

1 teaspoon **paprika**

½ teaspoon **ground ginger**

½ teaspoon **ground coriander**

½ teaspoon **ground turmeric**

¼ teaspoon **ground cinnamon**

¼ teaspoon **cayenne pepper**, plus more as needed

1 tablespoon **pomegranate seeds**

2 teaspoons chopped **fresh parsley**

Crackers, **pita chips**, or **sliced vegetables**, for serving

1. In the bowl of a food processor, process the torn pita until finely ground, about 1 minute. Add the red peppers, walnuts, scallions, chile, garlic, 3 tablespoons olive oil, the lemon zest and juice, 1 tablespoon pomegranate molasses, 1 teaspoon salt, the cumin, paprika, ginger, coriander, turmeric, cinnamon, and ¼ teaspoon cayenne and process until smooth, about 2 minutes, scraping down the sides of the bowl once or twice. Season to taste with more salt and cayenne.

2. Spoon the dip into a serving bowl and drizzle with more olive oil and pomegranate molasses. Garnish with the pomegranate seeds and parsley. Serve with crackers, pita chips, or veggies, or spread on your favorite sandwich.

firecracker chex mix

Tick, tick, tick, boom goes the dynamite! How do you possibly elevate Chex Mix? It isn't supposed to be fancy. In fact, the whole point of Chex Mix is to take supermarket ingredients, gussy them up a little, put them in a bowl, and get your fingers insanely dirty as you shovel fistfuls into your mouth. So, don't think of this as a "fancy Chex Mix," even though there's olive oil in it; think of it as a "better" Chex Mix. We've said good-bye to the packet of ranch dressing seasoning mix and in its place we have our own blend of garlic powder, lemon pepper, and sweet paprika, with red pepper flakes for heat. And just to prove this isn't fancy, we've added Goldfish crackers. Nothing fancy has Goldfish crackers in it! The defense rests.

~Jesse

1 cup **olive oil**

2 tablespoons **dried parsley**

2 teaspoons **red pepper flakes**, plus more as needed

2 teaspoons **garlic powder**

1 teaspoon **onion powder**

1 teaspoon **dried dill**

1 teaspoon **lemon pepper**

1¾ teaspoons **kosher salt**

½ teaspoon **paprika**

¼ teaspoon **freshly ground black pepper**

Pinch of **cayenne pepper** (optional)

⅓ cup **powdered buttermilk**

2 teaspoons **sugar**

4 cups **General Mills Rice** or **Corn Chex cereal**

2 cups **Pepperidge Farm Goldfish Cheddar Crackers** or **Annie's Cheddar Bunnies**

1. Preheat the oven to 300°F. Line a baking sheet with parchment paper.

2. In a large bowl, whisk together the oil, parsley, 2 teaspoons red pepper flakes, the garlic powder, onion powder, dill, lemon pepper, salt, paprika, pepper, cayenne, buttermilk powder, and sugar.

Add the cereal and crackers and toss to thoroughly coat.

3. Spread the mixture in an even layer on the baking sheet. Bake, gently tossing with a large spatula every few minutes to prevent burning, until the cereal starts to turn golden brown, about 15 minutes. Keep an eye on it, as it can burn

quickly! Remove from the oven and let cool completely on the baking sheet.

4. Transfer to an airtight container, scraping off any seasoning stuck to the parchment and tossing it with the mix. (The mix will keep in an airtight container at room temperature for up to 5 days.)

popcorn with everybay butter

Yes, you can buy fancy microwave popcorn with packaged seasoning. And yes, you can buy clarified butter in most grocery stores nowadays. But cooking your own popcorn and clarifying your own butter just gives better-tasting results. The process of clarifying butter is actually pretty calming, and it's a lot cheaper and less time-consuming than a yoga class. Our butter is seasoned with our EveryBay blend that is a riff on the classic Old Bay seasoning. ~**J&J**

2 tablespoons **clarified butter** (see page 262) or **canola oil**

½ cup **popcorn kernels**

2 tablespoons **EveryBay Butter** (page 262), warmed

Kosher salt

1. In a large, heavy-bottomed pot with a lid, heat the clarified butter and 2 popcorn kernels over medium heat until the kernels pop, 2 to 3 minutes. Reduce the heat to low and pour in the remaining kernels. Give the pot a swirl to coat the kernels in the hot butter. Cover the pot and let cook for about 1 minute. Increase the heat to medium and continue to cook, shaking the pot occasionally, until the kernels begin to pop. Slide the lid off just slightly to let steam escape and continue cooking until there are 2 to 3 seconds between pops, about 6 minutes total.

2. Transfer the popcorn to a large bowl. Drizzle with the EveryBay Butter, toss well, and season to taste with salt. Serve immediately.

bar snacks

As you can tell, the two of us have a love of bar snacks. Jesse once sat at a bar with his friend Eric, who kept eating the olives, candied ginger, and cherries the bartender had set up for making cocktails. When Jesse told him that they weren't for the customers to snack on, he was shocked. "Well, why would they put them on the edge of the bar right in front of us if they weren't for us to eat?" Jesse then commented that he thought olives, candied ginger, and cherries were a strange bar snack combination. "Well, I can't argue with that," Eric replied, as he popped a martini onion into his mouth. In this chapter, we've included some bar snacks you absolutely are allowed to eat.

eggplant chips

SERVES 4 TO 6

People in great marriages can be so cliché. "Being opposites totally works because we each bring something different to the relationship and we really complement each other." Ugh! We get it. However, that *is* how we feel about fried vegetables. Eggplant has a tendency to be a bit boring and a little soft, but in this preparation it just so happens to be married to a smoking hot thing called bread crumbs and oil! These "chips" are great just as they are, but if you wanted to dip them into something, we suggest the Alabama White BBQ Sauce (page 49). Great, now it's a thruple! ~ J&J

- 2 **Japanese eggplants** or **baby eggplants**, sliced into ¼-inch rounds
- 1 teaspoon **kosher salt**, plus more as needed
- 1 cup **all-purpose flour**
- 1 teaspoon **paprika**
- 3 large **eggs**
- 1⅓ cups **panko bread crumbs**
- ½ teaspoon **garlic powder**
- ½ teaspoon **onion powder**
- ¼ teaspoon **cayenne pepper**
- ½ teaspoon **dried oregano**
- ½ teaspoon **freshly ground black pepper**
- **Grapeseed** or **canola oil**
- **Alabama White BBQ Sauce** (page 49) or dip of choice

1. Arrange the eggplant slices in a single layer on a paper towel–lined baking sheet. Sprinkle both sides with the teaspoon of salt. Let sit for about 30 minutes, until some of the moisture is released. Blot dry with more paper towels.

2. In a shallow bowl, mix the flour and paprika. In another shallow bowl, lightly beat the eggs. In a third shallow bowl, combine the panko, garlic powder, onion powder, cayenne, oregano, and pepper. Coat the eggplant slices in the flour, then dip into the beaten eggs, then coat with the panko mixture.

3. Heat about ¼ inch of oil in a large cast-iron skillet over medium-high heat until shimmering. Working in batches, add the eggplant and fry for 2 to 3 minutes per side, until golden brown. Transfer to a paper towel–lined baking sheet to drain and immediately sprinkle with salt.

4. Serve the eggplant chips hot with the barbeque sauce or your dip of choice.

Clockwise from top: Crunchy, Dilly Pickled Beans; Firecracker Chex Mix; Eggplant Chips

crunchy, dilly pickled beans

Just pickle it! That's my solution when something is on its way out. I've made my love of salty pickling juices well known. In fact, "Pickle Juice Popsicles" was a recipe I really tried to get into this book.* Anyway, I love the union of dill and tarragon in this quick pickle. These beans are a great snack straight from the jar, but they also work brilliantly alongside a cheese spread or crudité platter. ~ Julie

- 3 sprigs of **fresh dill**
- 3 sprigs of **fresh tarragon**
- 1 pound fresh **green beans**, trimmed
- 1 cup **white wine vinegar**
- 1 cup **water**
- 1 tablespoon **sugar** or **honey**
- 1 tablespoon **kosher salt**
- 2 **garlic cloves**, smashed
- ½ teaspoon **white** or **black peppercorns**
- ½ teaspoon **coriander seeds**
- **Red pepper flakes** (optional)

1. Add the dill, tarragon, and green beans to a quart-sized glass jar with a lid. Cram them all in—they'll fit!

2. In a small saucepan, combine the vinegar, water, sugar, salt, garlic, peppercorns, coriander seeds, and red pepper flakes, if using. Bring to a boil over medium-high heat and cook until the sugar and salt have fully dissolved, 1 to 2 minutes. Pour the vinegar mixture over the green beans. Tightly seal the jar and let cool at room temperature for about 30 minutes. Transfer to the refrigerator to chill for at least 3 hours before serving. (These beans will keep in the refrigerator for a while. Actually, mine have been in the fridge for 6 weeks and I'm still eating them. Is that bad?)

*Psst: The recipe is just frozen pickle juice. There—I got it in!

"wtf is a sprig?"

This is what Jesse texted to me on May 10, 2020, 11:45 a.m.:

"I'm making the Crunchy, Dilly Pickled Beans and I feel like I need to address the elephant in the room: no one knows what a sprig is. Four sprigs? What does that *really* mean. Seriously, WTF is a 'sprig'? I'm eyeballing it. I don't care."

Google says a sprig is a 2- to 4-inch part of an herb plant, but I fully support Jesse's "eyeballing it" method.

orange–grapefruit julie-us

I wish I could have been a fly on the wall during the pitch meeting for the original Orange Julius: "Picture it: A hybrid of a fresh-squeezed OJ and a milkshake, served at a tiny juice shack. We will put one in every food court in America!" The concept seemed crazy, but I grew up hooked on Orange Julius. I don't know if I really want to know what was in the original recipe, but the internet is full of copycat versions, almost all of which call for frozen orange juice concentrate. We made it our mission to see if we could think up a fresh, all-natural version of this icy delight. Behold: The Orange-Grapefruit Julie-us!

Fresh orange and grapefruit juices stand in for the processed kind, and coconut milk brings a dairy-free creamy froth to the table. We celebrated our achievement by adding a shot (or two) of bourbon—something that definitely should have been mentioned in the original pitch meeting! ~ Julie

1 cup **fresh orange juice**

1 cup **fresh grapefruit juice**

1 cup canned **full-fat coconut milk**

¼ cup **confectioners' sugar**

2 tablespoons **honey**

1 teaspoon **vanilla extract**

1½ cups **ice cubes**

Bourbon (optional)

1. In a blender, combine the orange juice, grapefruit juice, coconut milk, confectioners' sugar, honey, vanilla, and ice cubes. Blend until smooth.

2. Divide the drink among four glasses. Add a shot or two of bourbon if it's been a long day.

Basil & Mint
Watermelon
Agua Fresca
and Orange-
Grapefruit
Julie-us

basil & mint watermelon agua fresca

Agua fresca, the juicy-watery drink of Mexico, translates to "cool water" or "fresh water." And these drinks are pretty damn refreshing! They taste a lot better than water, considering water tastes like wet air. There are tons of great combinations for a delicious fresca, and here we have one that bursts with summertime favorites. Light and cool, it's the perfect warm-weather drink; indeed, nothing reminds me of being at a pool more than watermelon. Making a simple syrup with the mint and basil leaves yields a prettier color in the end, but if you want to skip that step and don't mind a slightly "earthier color" (i.e., brown), then just add the mint and basil leaves along with the raw sugar and the rest of the ingredients into the blender and press "puree." If you are adding tequila or vodka, after a few drinks no one will even notice the slightly off-putting color. ~ **Jesse**

¼ cup **sugar**

½ cup **water**

10 to 12 **fresh basil leaves**, chopped

30 **fresh mint leaves**, chopped

6 cups cubed seedless **watermelon** (about 2 pounds)

Juice of 1½ **limes**

Pinch of **sea salt**

Ice cubes

Tequila or **vodka** (optional)

Soda water (optional)

1. In a small saucepan, combine the sugar and water. Bring to a simmer over medium-high heat, stirring to dissolve the sugar, about 3 minutes. Remove the pot from the heat and stir in the basil and mint. Let steep until the syrup cools completely, about 30 minutes.

2. Strain the syrup through a fine-mesh sieve into a blender, pressing on the herbs to extract as much syrup as possible. Discard the herbs. Add the watermelon, lime juice, and salt to the blender and blend until smooth. Strain through a fine-mesh sieve into a pitcher. (If you like a pulpier texture, skip the straining.)

3. Pour the agua fresca over ice cubes and add a shot of tequila, if you'd like. Top with soda water, if desired.

southern sweet tea

(WITH BOURBON)

Every year on my birthday, my best friend's mom would give me a pitcher of her sweet tea, along with a twenty-pound bedazzled, puffy sweatshirt she had painted. She'd even use some leftover ribbon from making the sweatshirt to tie a beautiful bow on the handle of the tea pitcher. It was my favorite gift! When I revisited her recipe for the tea, I realized it called for *way* more sugar than I remembered it having (twelve-year-old Julie loved her sugar). I've adapted my adult version to be a little less sweet to comply with my thirty-nine-year-old mom-of-two-kids-who-also-love-sugar taste buds. Don't worry; it's still sweet enough to live up to its name. (I also discovered that just a pinch of baking soda mellows the tannins in black tea, resulting in a smoother finish.) ~Julie

4 cups **boiling water**

4 black **tea bags** (such as Luzianne or Lipton)

⅛ teaspoon **baking soda**

¾ cup **sugar**

2 cups **ice water**

Lemon wedges and **mint sprigs,** for serving (optional)

Bourbon (optional)

1. Pour the boiling water into a large glass heatproof pitcher. Add the tea bags and baking soda, and gently stir to combine. Let the tea steep, uncovered, for 15 minutes. Remove the tea bags, discard, then stir in the sugar until dissolved. Pour in the ice water and stir to combine.

2. Chill the tea in the refrigerator for at least 1 hour before serving. Garnish each glass with a lemon wedge and a mint sprig, and add a shot of bourbon, if you'd like!

Drinks: (*noun*) Delicious, refreshing beverages that are often made with fresh juices, herbs, or sparkling waters. A popular favorite among people of all ages.

Dranks: (*noun*) Drinks containing booze. Traditionally enjoyed after the hour of 5 p.m., but oftentimes whenever one feels like it.

COCKTAILS
IN THE
LIBRARY?

cherry limeade

SERVES 4

(WITH VODKA)

If you look at the Southern Sweet Tea recipe (page 252), it won't surprise you that Julie is a sugar pusher. She goes to bat for it with the same passion as I campaign for agave. I love using agave syrup (also known as agave nectar) to sweeten drinks instead of a simple syrup made with cane sugar. I just think it tastes better. Now, don't get me wrong; I love sugar, but the addition of cherry juice here more than makes up for it! However, we have given you the option to use, either. Call it the Julie Method vs. the Jesse Method. ~ Jesse

½ cup **agave syrup** or **sugar**
½ cup **water**
1 (2-inch) piece of **fresh ginger**, roughly chopped
Finely grated zest from 1 **lime**
1 cup **fresh lime juice** (from 8 to 10 limes), plus lime wedges, for serving

2 cups **soda water**
1 (9-ounce) jar **maraschino cherries** (about 15 cherries), plus 4 to 6 tablespoons juice (or **grenadine syrup**)
Ice cubes
Vodka (optional)

1. In a small saucepan set over medium-high heat, stir together the agave syrup, water, ginger, and lime zest. Cook until the syrup has blended with the water, about 2 minutes. Remove from the heat, cover, and allow the syrup to steep at room temperature for 20 minutes.

2. Strain the syrup into a large pitcher. Add the lime juice, soda water, cherries, and 4 tablespoons of the cherry juice, and stir to combine. Taste and adjust flavoring with additional juice, if desired. Refrigerate until ice cold.

3. To serve, pour the mixture over ice cubes (along with a shot of vodka, if desired) and add a lime wedge to each glass.

marga–reenie

(BEER
MARGARITA)

One of my best friends in New York City, Colin Hanlon, introduced me to this boozy delight. The Hanlon family, who lived a short train ride from the city in the suburbs of Philadelphia, would always open their door to me on the holidays, when I couldn't afford to travel back home to New Mexico. Their household always seemed to be the gathering spot for the extended family, so over various Christmases, Thanksgivings, and Easters I got to know their relatives pretty well. The trouble always started when Aunt Reenie whipped up her first batch of beer margaritas. Colin, his sister Kelly, and I would share a "we are in this together" look before accepting the first of what would inevitably be several glasses of Marga-Reenies. This three-ingredient booze bomb can literally be made in 30 seconds. Truly, we timed Reenie once.

We really recommend using frozen juice here. (The can also doubles as a disposable measuring cup.) The recipe has the equivalent of one shot, or 1.5 ounces (3 tablespoons), of tequila per serving. But you can make this virgin by leaving out the beer and the tequila. Just follow the instructions on the can; it's called limeade. ~ Jesse

1 (12-ounce) can frozen **limeade concentrate**

1 (12-ounce) bottle **amber beer** or **light beer of choice**

12 ounces (1½ cups) **silver tequila**

Kosher salt, for rimming the glasses (optional)

Lime wedges, for serving

1. Empty the can of limeade concentrate into a large pitcher. Add the beer. Fill the limeade can with tequila, then add that to the pitcher. Fill the can with water (thank God!) and dump that in, too. Stir. Done.

2. Pour over ice cubes in salt-rimmed glasses, if desired, and serve with lime wedges. Partake of extra water for hydration between the margaritas; that's a lesson that took me a surprisingly long time to figure out.

you deserve butter ~by Julie

Runners up for the title of this chapter were "Butter Together," "My Butter Half," and "Butter from Another Udder." I'm indecisive; it's Jesse's favorite quality about me.

I loved butter so much when I was growing up that I would just eat it plain. I didn't need a biscuit or cracker, just plain butter. Surprisingly, my parents weren't bothered by my consumption of straight butter. They were, however, annoyed with my technique of consuming it. I'd open the refrigerator, climb up on a step stool, lift the lid off the butter dish, and carve out little bits with my fingernail. Every time my parents confronted me about it, I suggested that we had a mouse. Yes, a mouse that had opposable thumbs and the upper-body strength to open a refrigerator door. Seemed logical at the time.

I remember when I was in culinary school, my favorite chef-instructor talked about her love for butter and then informed us that the fat in butter is good for brain development. I remember thinking, "My love affair doesn't have to be a secret anymore! I eat butter with my fingers!" Here, I get to share my love of butter and some of my favorite ways to use it! I've presented recipes for clarified, browned, infused (stuff cooked in), and compound (stuff mixed in) butters.

In fact, butter is front and center in a lot of the recipes in this book. Just think of the smell of onions sautéing in a rich browning butter. There should be no shame in loving this perfect ingredient—even if you are like me and enjoy eating it raw. She is essential and irreplaceable. (Yes, like God, butter is a woman.)

clarified butter

The process of drawing the milk solids out of butter leaves a golden-hued fat with a higher smoking point, making it an ideal stand-in for oil. It's perfect for sautéing and popping popcorn. This is more of a technique than a recipe, so use as much butter as you want.

Add cubed butter to a small saucepan. Melt it over low heat without disturbing it and bring to a gentle simmer (do not let it come to a full boil), about 30 minutes. The milk solids will rise to the surface as foamy bubbles; skim them off with a ladle or spoon, and transfer to a bowl (see Note). Once all the milk solids have been removed, the remaining clarified butter will be dark yellow and mostly clear. If a lot of milk solids fall to the bottom of your pot, simply strain the butter through a fine-mesh sieve. Transfer the clarified butter to a glass jar and store in the refrigerator for up to 1 month.

notes

Don't toss out those milk solids! Brown them in a skillet and add to cookies, mashed potatoes, grits, biscuits, and the like.

Compound (flavored) butters can be stored in the refrigerator for about 1 week or in the freezer for about 3 months. There are several different ways you can store your homemade butters:

Wrapped: Wrap your butter in plastic wrap or parchment paper and roll into a log.

Butter keeper: Press the butter into small ramekins or bowls. You can also get fancy and buy an official butter keeper. There are tons of cute varieties available.

Mason jar: Clarified butters and other softer butters can be stored in a mason jar in the fridge.

everybay butter

MAKES ABOUT ⅓ CUP

Delicious drizzled over a delicate fish or roasted vegetables or tossed with popcorn for a special movie night.

EVERYBAY SEASONING
- 1 tablespoon plus 2 teaspoons **celery salt**
- 1 tablespoon plus 1 teaspoon **paprika**
- 2 teaspoons ground **dried bay leaves**
- 1½ teaspoons **dry mustard**
- 1½ teaspoons **ground sumac**
- 1 teaspoon **black pepper**
- ½ teaspoon **ground ginger**
- ½ teaspoon **smoked paprika**
- ½ teaspoon **ground white pepper**
- ½ teaspoon **cayenne pepper**
- ¼ teaspoon **ground allspice**

BUTTER
- 1 teaspoon **dried minced onion**
- ½ cup **clarified butter** (at left)

1. **Make the seasoning:** In a small resealable container, combine the celery salt, paprika, ground bay leaves, dry mustard, sumac, black pepper, ginger, smoked paprika, white pepper, cayenne, and allspice. Cover and shake well to distribute. (The dry spice mix will keep at room temperature for 1 year.)

2. **Make the butter:** Stir 1½ tablespoons of the seasoning mix and the minced onion into the warm clarified butter. Transfer to a glass jar and store in the refrigerator for up to 1 month.

brown butter

MAKES ABOUT ⅓ CUP

Cooking butter a little hotter than enough to clarify it allows you to brown the milk solids, leaving you with a rich, nutty browned butter, ideal for adding depth to everything from savory dishes (like our Charred Brussels Sprouts with Brown Butter Vinaigrette, page 166) to baked goods, like cookies or pancakes.

½ cup (1 stick) **unsalted butter**, cut into dice

Melt the butter in a small saucepan over medium heat. Cook, stirring often, until the milk solids have browned but not burned, and the butter smells nutty, 6 to 8 minutes. Transfer to a glass jar and use immediately, or let cool. (Can be stored in a glass jar in the refrigerator for up to 2 weeks.)

lemony sorghum brown butter

MAKES ABOUT 1 CUP

This rich butter tastes like a lemon bar, and I want to drizzle it all over my life—or at least into the Roasted Sweet Potato Soup (page 185).

½ cup (1 stick) **unsalted butter**, cut into dice
Juice of 2 **lemons**
¼ cup **sorghum syrup**
¼ teaspoon **kosher salt**

Melt the butter in a small saucepan over medium heat. Cook, stirring often, until the milk solids have browned but not burned, and the butter smells nutty, 6 to 8 minutes. Remove the pan from the heat and immediately whisk in the lemon juice, sorghum syrup, and salt. (Store in a glass jar in the fridge for up to 2 weeks.)

sorghum butter

MAKES ABOUT ¾ CUP

This sweetened butter can both handle the simple task of buttering a biscuit and bring caramelized crispiness to Sorghum Butter Spatchcocked Chicken (page 71).

½ cup (1 stick) **unsalted butter**, room temperature
3 tablespoons **sorghum syrup**
¾ teaspoon **paprika**
Pinch of **kosher salt**

In a small bowl, stir together the softened butter, sorghum syrup, paprika, and salt. (Store it in the fridge, wrapped in paper or plastic, or in a butter keeper, for up to 2 weeks.)

chipotle lime butter

MAKES ABOUT 1 CUP

This rich, smoky butter with a kick is our favorite way to punch up a ribeye steak (see page 98) or baked potato.

½ cup (1 stick) **unsalted butter**, room temperature
2 tablespoons chopped **fresh cilantro**
Finely grated zest of 1 **lime**
4 teaspoons fresh **lime juice**
2 canned **chipotle chiles in adobo sauce**, finely chopped
½ teaspoon **kosher salt**

In a medium bowl, whip the softened butter with a fork until light and fluffy. Add the cilantro, lime zest and juice, chipotle chiles, and salt and stir to combine. (Store in the fridge, wrapped in paper or plastic, or in a butter keeper, for up to 5 days; or freeze for up to 3 months.)

blueberry butter

Great antioxidant, decreases inflammation, promotes a healthy heart—yeah, yeah, yeah. *Our* love of blueberries is rooted in its perfect balance between tart and sweet. This butter brings an extra hue of cerulean to the Blue Cornmeal Pancakes (page 21), but it also happens to be our favorite butter for muffins or scones.

½ cup (1 stick) **unsalted butter**, room temperature
¼ cup **fresh blueberries**, washed and thoroughly dried
2 teaspoons **blueberry preserves**
¼ teaspoon **ground coriander**
Pinch of **kosher salt**

Add the butter, blueberries, preserves, coriander, and salt to a food processor. Blend until smooth. (Store in the fridge, wrapped in paper or plastic, or in a butter keeper, for up to 5 days; or freeze for up to 3 months.)

tip

Room-Temperature Butter: A stick of butter coming out of the fridge can take a surprisingly long time to come to room temperature. To speed it up, cut the butter into ½-inch pieces and leave on the counter; it should be at room temp in 10 to 12 minutes.

walnut–honey butter

If you are the type of person who bypasses the creamy Jif for the crunchy variety, this butter is for you! It's delicious on pancakes, waffles (see page 36), or pastries.

½ cup **walnut halves** or **pieces**
½ cup (1 stick) **unsalted butter**, room temperature
1½ teaspoons **honey**
¼ teaspoon **ground cinnamon**
Pinch of **flaky sea salt**

1. Toast the walnuts in a small, dry skillet until golden brown and fragrant, about 8 minutes. Transfer to a cutting board and finely chop.

2. In a medium bowl, whip the softened butter with a fork until light and fluffy. Stir in the honey, cinnamon, and salt, then fold in the chopped walnuts. (Store in the fridge, wrapped in paper or plastic, or in a butter keeper, for up to 2 weeks.)

acknowledgments

If not for you . . .

You guys, writing a cookbook is a LOT of work and we wouldn't have been able to do it without our two biggest cheerleaders—our husbands, Justin Mikita and Will Tanous. Somehow, they could always see the light at the end of the tunnel, and through their patience, love, and encouragement they kept reminding us that we could do this!

To our friends, family members, mentors, collaborators, and advisors who contributed in some way to the creation of this book. Thank you to everyone listed here for your support, talent, loyalty, creativity, and wisdom. As Dylan wrote, without your love we'd be nowhere at all.

Justin Chapple
Sarah Carey
Ellen Bennett
Chrissy Teigen
Padma Lakshmi
Teri Turner
Adam Roberts
Gail Simmons
Fred Wistow
Brian Hart-Hoffman
Adeena Sussman
Natasha Phan
Jen Joel
Kari Stuart
Bonnie Bernstein

Craig Gartner
Francis Lam
Lydia O'Brien
Amanda Englander
Stephanie Huntwork
Jennifer K. Beal Davis
Derek Gullino
Mark McCauslin
Neil Spitkovsky
Merri Ann Morrell
Zoe Tokushige
Eva Kolenko
Marian Cooper Cairns
Natasha Kolenko
Annie Psaltiras

Jessica Elbaum
Andrew Zepeda
Mary Inacio
Maggie Mariolis
Danielle DeLott
Ted Rosen
Farideh Sadeghin
Deenie Hartzog-Mislock
Lindsey Marie Miles
Corene Phillips (aka Coco)
Jim Phillips
Isabella Bartilucci
Maria Sanchez
Heather Brewer
Todd Hawkins

Ryan Crampton
Kevin Rutkowski
Ariel Lawrence
Robert Ferguson
Anne Ferguson
Muriel Vega
Mike Mikita
Kris Mikita
Leticia Lopez
Sofia Gutierrez
Don Collins
Janet Gomez
Bryan Godwin
Mary Jane Waldrop
Ella Huber

To all the chefs we've loved before . . .

Even though they were not involved in the making of this book, without knowing it, these chefs are part of its DNA. We have learned so much about their cultures through the food they have made for us and the recipes they have published. We firmly believe that feeding one another blurs the borders of our

world, and the sharing of our ancestry and histories, both painful and joyful, only brings us closer together. These are just some of the many people who have inspired us to commit to learning more, to make our table bigger, and to celebrate each other's traditions.

Enrique Olvera
Daniela Soto-Innes
Tanya Holland
Susan Feniger
Rick Bayless
Jonathan Perno
Art Smith

José Andrés
Sarah Kramer
Sarah Hymanson
Carla Hall
Nancy Silverton
Roy Choi
Sean Brock

Frank Stitt
Dolester Miles
Ashley Christensen
Edna Lewis
Michael Twitty
David Chang
Martha Stewart

Candace Nelson
Kristen Kish
Toni Tipton-Martin
Missy Robbins
Ludo Lefebvre
And, yes, our moms,
Coco and Anne

index